REAL ESTATE INVESTING ON A BUDGET 2024

TIPS ON HOW TO GET STARTED WITH LITTLE OR NO MONEY DOWN

TYLER GIBSON

CONTENTS

Chapter 1: Introduction to Real Estate Investing on a Budget

1.1. What is real estate investing?

Real estate investing is the purchase, management, and sale or rental of real estate for profit. It is a broad category that encompasses a variety of different strategies, including:

1. **Fix-and-flip investing:** Buying distressed properties, renovating them, and selling them for a profit.
2. **Rental property investing:** Buying properties to rent out to tenants.
3. **Real estate syndications:** Pooling money with other investors to buy and manage large real estate projects.
4. **Real estate crowdfunding:** Investing in real estate projects through online platforms.
5. **Real estate investment trusts (REITs):** Investing in companies that own and operate income-producing real estate.

Real estate investing can be a great way to build wealth over time. It is a tangible asset that can be appreciated in value, and it can provide a steady stream of income from rent payments. However, it is important to remember that real estate investing is also a risky investment. There is always the potential to lose money, especially if you do not do your research and make sound investment decisions.

Here are some of the key things to consider when investing in real estate:

1. Location: The location of a property is one of the most important factors to consider when investing in real estate. Properties in desirable locations with strong economies are more likely to appreciate value and generate higher rental income.

2. Property type: There are different types of real estate, including residential, commercial, and industrial properties. Each type of property has its own advantages and disadvantages. For example, residential properties can be more difficult to manage than commercial properties, but they can also generate higher rental income.

3. Investment strategy: What are your goals for your real estate investment? Are you looking for a long-term investment that will increase in value over time? Or are you looking for a short-term investment that will generate cash flow quickly? Your investment strategy will determine the type of property you purchase and the way you manage it.

4. Financing: Real estate investing can be expensive, so it is important to have a financing plan in place. There are a variety of different financing options available, including traditional mortgages, private loans, and hard money loans.

5. Risk tolerance: Real estate investing is a risky investment, so it is important to understand your risk tolerance before you invest. How much money can you afford to lose? How long are you willing to hold your investment? Your risk tolerance will help you determine the type of investment strategy that is right for you.

If you are considering investing in real estate, it is important to do your research and understand the risks involved. It is also a good idea to talk to a financial advisor to get personalized advice.

Here are some of the benefits and risks of real estate investing:

Benefits:

1. **Potential for high returns:** Real estate has the potential to generate high returns on investment, both through appreciation and rental income.
2. **Tangible asset:** Real estate is a tangible asset that you can see and touch. This can make it a more appealing investment than some other types of investments, such as stocks and bonds.
3. **Tax benefits:** Real estate investors can qualify for a variety of tax benefits, such as depreciation deductions and mortgage interest deductions.
4. **Hedge against inflation:** Real estate can be a good hedge against inflation, as the value of real estate tends to rise over time.

Risks:

1. **High upfront costs:** Real estate can be a very expensive investment, especially if you are buying a property with a down payment.
2. **Illiquidity:** Real estate is an illiquid asset, meaning that it can be difficult to sell quickly if you need to.
3. **Vacancy risk:** If you are renting out your property, there is always the risk that you will have a vacancy period when you are not receiving any rental income.
4. **Maintenance and repairs:** Real estate can require ongoing maintenance and repairs, which can be costly.
5. **Market risk:** The value of real estate can fluctuate depending on the market. If the market takes a downturn, you may lose money on your investment.

Overall, real estate investing can be a great way to build wealth over time. However, it is important to understand the risks involved before you invest.

1.2. Why invest in real estate?

There are many reasons why real estate can be a good investment. Here are a few of the most common:

1. Potential for appreciation: Over time, real estate tends to appreciate in value. This is due to a number of factors, including population growth, inflation, and limited land supply. When you invest in real estate, you have the potential to sell your property for more than you paid for it, generating a capital gain.

2. Passive income: Real estate can also provide a source of passive income. When you rent out a property, you generate income each month without having to actively work for it. This can be a great way to supplement your regular income or even to create a full-time income from real estate.

3. Tax benefits: Real estate investors can enjoy a number of tax benefits. For example, you can deduct mortgage interest, property taxes, and depreciation expenses from your taxable income. This can help to reduce your overall tax bill.

4. Hedge against inflation: Real estate can also be a good hedge against inflation. When inflation rises, the value of real estate tends to rise as well. This is because real estate is a hard asset, meaning that it has a physical value that is not easily impacted by inflation.

5. Leverage: Real estate investors can use leverage to finance their investments. This means that you can borrow money to buy properties, which allows you to control more assets than you could if you were paying for them all in cash. However, it is important to use leverage carefully, as it can also amplify your losses if the market turns down.

In addition to these general benefits, real estate can also offer several specific benefits depending on the type of property you invest in. For example, investing in commercial real estate can provide you with a steady stream of income from tenants. Investing in residential real estate can allow you to flip houses for a profit or to rent out properties to tenants.

Real estate is not without its risks, however. One of the biggest risks is that the market can turn down. If the market is down, it can be difficult to sell your property for a profit. Additionally, real estate can be an illiquid asset, meaning that it can be difficult to sell quickly if you need cash.

Overall, real estate can be a good investment for people who are looking for a long-term investment with the potential for appreciation, passive income, and tax benefits. However, it is important to understand the risks involved before investing in real estate.

Here are some additional things to consider when deciding whether or not to invest in real estate:

1. **Your financial situation:** Real estate investing can be a capital-intensive investment. You will need to have a down payment saved up, as well as enough money to cover closing costs and other expenses. You will also need to be able to qualify for a mortgage loan.
2. **Your investment goals:** What are you hoping to achieve with your real estate investment? Are you looking for a long-term investment with the potential

for appreciation? Are you looking for a source of passive income? Are you looking to flip houses for a profit?

3. **Your risk tolerance:** Real estate investing is not without its risks. The market can turn down, and it can be difficult to sell your property quickly if you need cash. Are you comfortable with the risks involved?

4. **Your time commitment:** Real estate investing can be a time-consuming activity. You will need to research the market, find properties, negotiate deals, and manage your properties. Are you willing to put in the time and effort required to be a successful real estate investor?

1.3. The benefits of investing in real estate on a budget

Investing in real estate can be a great way to build wealth over time, but it can also be a daunting prospect, especially if you're on a budget. However, there are several ways to invest in real estate on a budget, and there are several potential benefits to doing so.

One of the biggest benefits of investing in real estate on a budget is that it can help you build equity more quickly. When you buy a property with a low-down payment, you'll have a higher mortgage-to-equity ratio. However, as you make mortgage payments, you'll be building equity in your property. This equity can be used to leverage future investments or to tap into cash flow.

Another benefit of investing in real estate on a budget is that it can provide you with a source of passive income. When you rent out a property, you're essentially creating a business that generates income regularly. This income can be used to offset the costs of your mortgage, or it can be used to supplement your other income streams.

In addition, investing in real estate on a budget can be a great way to hedge against inflation. Over time, the value of real estate tends to appreciate, which means that your investment is likely to become more valuable over time. This can be a great way to protect your wealth from the effects of inflation.

Finally, investing in real estate on a budget can be a great way to build your financial future. By building equity and generating passive income, you can create a strong foundation for your financial future. This can help you to achieve your financial goals, such as saving for retirement or buying a larger home.

1.4. How to get started with real estate investing on a budget

To get started with real estate investing on a budget, there are a few key things you need to do:

1. Educate yourself. The more you know about real estate investing, the better equipped you will be to make sound investment decisions. There are many resources available to help you learn about real estate investing, including books, websites, and courses.

2. Get your finances in order. Before you start investing in real estate, you need to make sure your finances are in order. This means having a good credit score, a steady income, and enough savings to cover your down payment and closing costs.

3. Choose a real estate investment strategy. There are many different ways to invest in real estate, such as buying and flipping properties, renting out properties, or investing in real estate trusts (REITs). Choose an investment strategy that is right for your experience level, budget, and risk tolerance.

4. Find the right properties. Once you have chosen a real estate investment strategy, you need to start finding the right properties to invest in. This can be done by working with a real estate agent, searching online listings, or networking with other investors.

5. Secure financing. Unless you have enough cash to buy a property outright, you will need to secure financing. There are many different types of financing available for real estate investors, such as traditional mortgages, hard money loans, and private loans.

Here are some specific tips for getting started with real estate investing on a budget:

1. Consider creative financing strategies. There are a number of creative financing strategies that can help you invest in real estate with little or no money down. For example, you could partner with another investor, use a seller financing arrangement, or get a hard money loan.

2. Start small. You don't need to buy a multi-million-dollar mansion to get started with real estate investing. You could start by investing in a single-family home, a duplex, or even a fourplex.

3. Focus on undervalued properties. Look for properties that are selling below market value. This could be due to a number of factors, such as the property needing repairs or being located in an up-and-coming neighborhood.

4. Be patient. It takes time to build a successful real estate investment portfolio. Don't expect to get rich quick. Instead, focus on making smart investments over time.

Here are some additional tips for real estate investing on a budget:

1. Network with other investors. Networking with other real estate investors is a great way to learn from their experiences and find investment opportunities.

2. Use technology to your advantage. There are a number of online resources that can help you find investment properties, secure financing, and manage your investments.

3. Don't be afraid to ask for help. If you need help with any aspect of real estate investing, don't be afraid to ask for help from a real estate agent, attorney, or accountant.

Real estate investing can be a great way to build wealth over time, but it is important to remember that it is also a risky investment. Before you invest in real estate, make sure you understand the risks involved and that you have a solid financial plan in place.

Chapter 2: Understanding the Real Estate Market

2.1. The different types of real estate investments

There are many different types of real estate investments, each with its own unique benefits and risks. Some of the most common types of real estate investments include:

1. Residential real estate: Residential real estate includes single-family homes, multi-family homes, and townhomes. Residential real estate can be a good investment because it is a relatively tangible asset that can generate income through rent or appreciation. However, residential real estate can also be an illiquid asset, meaning that it can be difficult to sell quickly.

2. Commercial real estate: Commercial real estate includes office buildings, retail centers, industrial properties, and hotels. Commercial real estate can be a good investment because it can generate higher returns than residential real estate. However, commercial real estate is also a more complex and risky investment than residential real estate.

3. Land: Land can be a good investment because it is a scarce resource that can appreciate in value over time. However, land is also an illiquid asset and can be difficult to generate income from.

4. Real estate investment trusts (REITs): REITs are companies that own and operate income-producing real estate assets. REITs can be a good way to invest in real estate without having to purchase and manage properties directly. However, REITs are subject to the same risks as other stocks, such as market volatility.

5. Real estate crowdfunding: Real estate crowdfunding platforms allow investors to pool their money to invest in real estate projects. Real estate crowdfunding can be a good way to invest in real estate with a smaller investment amount. However, real estate crowdfunding is also a relatively new and risky investment.

In addition to these general types of real estate investments, there are also a number of specialized real estate investments, such as:

1. Fix-and-flip properties: Fix-and-flip properties are properties that are purchased below market value, renovated, and then sold for a profit. Fix-and-flip properties can be a good investment for experienced investors, but they can also be risky for inexperienced investors.

2. Rental properties: Rental properties are properties that are purchased and then rented out to tenants. Rental properties can be a good way to generate income and build wealth over time. However, rental properties also require a significant amount of work and management.

3. Vacation rentals: Vacation rentals are properties that are rented out to tourists on a short-term basis. Vacation rentals can be a good way to generate income, but they can also be seasonal and require a significant amount of work and management.

The best type of real estate investment for you will depend on your individual investment goals, risk tolerance, and budget. It is important to do your research and understand the risks involved before making any real estate investment.

Here are some additional considerations when choosing a type of real estate investment:

1. Location: The location of the property is one of the most important factors to consider when choosing a real estate investment. Properties in desirable locations are more likely to appreciate in value and generate higher rental income.

2. Condition: The condition of the property is also an important factor to consider. Properties in need of significant repairs or renovations may require a larger upfront investment, but they may also have more potential for appreciation.

3. Cash flow: If you are looking for an investment that will generate immediate income, you may want to consider a rental property. However, it is important to factor in the costs of owning and managing a rental property, such as mortgage payments, property taxes, and maintenance costs.

4. Appreciation: If you are looking for an investment that will appreciate in value over time, you may want to consider a property in a desirable location or a property that is in need of renovations.

2.2. How to assess the value of a property

To assess the value of a property, you need to consider a variety of factors, including:

1. Location: The location of a property is one of the most important factors that determines its value. Properties in desirable neighborhoods with good schools, amenities, and job opportunities will typically be worth more than properties in less desirable areas.

2. Property condition: The overall condition of a property will also affect its value. Properties that are in good condition and have been well-maintained will be worth more than properties that are in need of repairs or renovations.

3. Property features: The specific features of a property, such as the number of bedrooms and bathrooms, square footage, and lot size, will also affect its value. Properties with more bedrooms and bathrooms, larger square footage, and larger lots will typically be worth more.

4. Recent sales data: One of the best ways to assess the value of a property is to look at recent sales data for similar properties in the same area. This will give you a good idea of what buyers are willing to pay for similar properties.

There are three main approaches to assessing the value of a property:

1. Sales comparison approach: This approach compares the property to similar properties that have recently sold in the same area. The sales comparison approach is the most common approach used to assess the value of residential real estate.

2. Cost approach: This approach estimates the cost of replacing the property, minus depreciation. The cost approach is often used to assess the value of commercial real estate and properties that are difficult to find comparable sales for.

3. Income approach: This approach estimates the value of a property based on its income-generating potential. The income approach is often used to assess the value of investment properties, such as rental properties and office buildings.

Which approach you use to assess the value of a property will depend on the type of property and the availability of data. For example, if you are assessing the value of a single-family home, you will likely use the sales comparison approach. If you are assessing the value of a commercial property, you may use the cost approach or the income approach.

If you are serious about buying or selling real estate, it is important to have a professional appraiser assess the value of the property. A professional appraiser is trained and experienced in using all three approaches to assess the value of property. They will also have access to data that you may not have access to, such as recent sales data for comparable properties.

Here are some additional tips for assessing the value of a property:

1. Consider the future potential of the area. If the property is located in an area that is expected to grow or develop in the future, this could increase its value.
2. Look for unique features. If the property has unique features, such as a water view or a pool, this could also increase its value.
3. Consider the condition of the local real estate market. If the local real estate market is hot, this could drive up the value of the property. However, if the local real estate market is slow, this could drive down the value of the property.

By considering all of these factors, you can get a good idea of the value of a property. However, it is important to keep in mind that the value of a property is ultimately determined by what a buyer is willing to pay for it.

2.3. How to find the right investment properties

Finding the right investment properties is essential to success in real estate investing. There are a number of factors to consider when choosing an investment property, including:

1. Location: The location of a property is one of the most important factors to consider. Look for properties in areas with a strong economy, good schools, and low crime rates. You should also consider the proximity to amenities such as shopping, dining, and transportation.

2. Property type: There are a variety of different types of investment properties, including single-family homes, multi-family homes, commercial properties, and industrial properties. Choose a property type that is well-suited to your investment goals and risk tolerance.

3. Condition of the property: The condition of the property is another important factor to consider. Consider the age of the property, any repairs or renovations that need to be made, and the overall condition of the building and grounds.

4. Price: It is important to find a property that is priced fairly and that will generate a positive return on investment. You should factor in all of the costs associated with owning and operating the property, including mortgage payments, property taxes, insurance, and maintenance costs.

Once you have considered these factors, you can start your search for investment properties. There are a number of ways to find investment properties, including:

1. Working with a real estate agent: A real estate agent can help you find properties that meet your investment criteria and negotiate the best possible price.

2. Searching online listings: There are a number of websites that list investment properties for sale. You can search by location, property type, and other criteria.

3. Attending real estate auctions: Real estate auctions can be a great way to find investment properties at below-market prices.

4. Networking with other real estate investors: Networking with other real estate investors is a great way to learn about off-market deals and other investment opportunities.

Once you have found a few potential investment properties, it is important to do your due diligence before making an offer. This includes conducting a thorough property inspection, reviewing the financial statements of the property, and understanding the zoning laws and other regulations that apply to the property.

Here are some additional tips for finding the right investment properties:

1. Focus on a specific niche. It is helpful to focus on a specific niche in real estate investing, such as single-family homes in a particular neighborhood or commercial properties in a growing area. This will help you to become an expert in your chosen niche and to identify the best investment opportunities.
2. Be prepared to act quickly. The real estate market can be very competitive, so it is important to be prepared to act quickly when you find a good deal. Make sure that you have your financing in place and that you are ready to make an offer.

3. Don't be afraid to negotiate. Once you have made an offer, be prepared to negotiate with the seller. Try to get the best possible price and terms for the property.

Finding the right investment properties takes time and effort, but it is essential to success in real estate investing. By following the tips above, you can increase your chances of finding properties that will generate positive returns on your investment.

2.4. How to finance your real estate investments

There are a variety of ways to finance real estate investments, and the best option for you will depend on your individual financial situation and investment goals. Here are some of the most common financing options:

1. Conventional bank loans: Conventional bank loans are the most common type of financing for real estate investments. To qualify for a conventional bank loan, you will typically need a down payment of at least 20% of the purchase price of the property. You will also need a good credit score and a steady income.

2. Hard money loans: Hard money loans are short-term loans that are typically used to finance fix-and-flip properties. Hard money loans can be obtained from private lenders, and they typically have higher interest rates and shorter repayment terms than conventional bank loans.

3. Private money loans: Private money loans are loans that are obtained from individuals, such as friends, family, or business associates. Private money loans can be a good option for investors who do not qualify for a conventional bank loan or who need financing quickly.

4. Home equity loans: Home equity loans allow you to borrow money against the equity in your primary residence. Home equity loans can be used to finance investment properties, but they should be used with caution, as you could risk losing your home if you are unable to repay the loan.

5. Real estate investment trusts (REITs): REITs are companies that own and operate income-producing real estate. REITs are traded on public exchanges, and they can be a good way to invest in real estate without having to purchase individual properties.

In addition to these traditional financing options, there are also a number of creative financing strategies that investors can use. For example, some investors use lease-to-own agreements to purchase investment properties. Lease-to-own agreements allow investors to lease a property with the option to purchase it at a later date. This can be a good option for investors who do not have a large down payment or who need time to improve their credit scores.

Other investors use seller financing to purchase investment properties. Seller financing allows investors to purchase a property directly from the seller without having to obtain a loan from a bank. This can be a good option for investors who are purchasing a property from a motivated seller.

No matter what financing option you choose, it is important to carefully consider your financial situation and investment goals before making a decision. You should also consult with a financial advisor to get personalized advice.

Here are some additional tips for financing your real estate investments:

1. Get pre-approved for a loan before you start shopping for properties. This will give you an idea of how much money you can borrow and what your monthly payments will be.
2. Shop around for the best interest rates and terms. Compare offers from multiple lenders before you choose a loan.
3. Consider using a mortgage broker. A mortgage broker can help you find the best loan for your needs and can negotiate on your behalf.
4. Make a larger down payment if possible. A larger down payment will reduce your monthly payments and will also give you more equity in the property.
5. Have a plan for how you will repay your loan. Make sure you can afford the monthly payments and that you have a plan in place in case of unexpected expenses.

Chapter 3: Creative Financing Strategies for Real Estate Investors

3.1. How to buy real estate with no money down

Buying real estate with no money down is possible, but it is not easy. It requires creativity, hustle, and a willingness to take risks. There are a number of different ways to do it, but the most common methods include:

1. Seller financing

Seller financing is when the seller of the property agrees to finance the purchase for the buyer. This means that the buyer does not need to go through a traditional lender to get a mortgage. Seller financing is often more flexible than a traditional mortgage, and it can be a good option for buyers with bad credit or no down payment.

To find a seller who is willing to offer seller financing, you can work with a real estate agent who specializes in seller-financed deals. You can also search online for properties that are listed for sale by owner.

2. USDA loans

USDA loans are government-backed loans that are available to buyers in rural areas. USDA loans do not require a down payment, and they have competitive interest rates. To qualify for a USDA loan, your household income must meet certain requirements, and the property you are buying must be located in a USDA-eligible area.

3. VA loans

VA loans are government-backed loans that are available to veterans and their spouses. VA loans do not require a down payment, and they have competitive interest rates. To qualify for a VA loan, you must meet certain service requirements.

4. FHA loans

FHA loans are government-backed loans that are available to borrowers with lower credit scores. FHA loans require a down payment of as little as 3.5%.

5. Hard money loans

Hard money loans are private loans that are typically used to finance short-term real estate deals. Hard money loans have higher interest rates than traditional mortgages, but they can be a good option for buyers who need to close quickly or who have bad credit.

6. Lease-purchase options

A lease-purchase option is an agreement between a buyer and a seller that gives the buyer the right to purchase the property at a future date for a predetermined price. The buyer pays a lease payment to the seller each month, and a portion of the lease payment goes towards the down payment.

7. Creative financing strategies

There are a number of other creative financing strategies that can be used to buy real estate with no money down. For example, you could partner with another investor, or you could raise money from private investors.

Tips for buying real estate with no money down

Here are a few tips for buying real estate with no money down:

1. Do your research. Before you start looking for properties, it is important to understand the different financing options available to you.
2. Work with a qualified real estate agent. A good real estate agent can help you find properties that are eligible for seller financing or other no-money-down financing options.
3. Be prepared to negotiate. When you are buying real estate with no money down, it is important to be prepared to negotiate with sellers. Be willing to compromise on price or other terms in order to get the deal done.
4. Have a backup plan. In case you are unable to find a seller who is willing to offer seller financing or you do not qualify for a USDA, VA, or FHA loan, it is important to have a backup plan. This could include having a down payment saved up or having a cosigner who is willing to sign on your mortgage.

3.2. How to use leverage to finance your real estate investments

Leverage is the use of borrowed money to finance an investment. In real estate investing, leverage is often used to purchase properties with a smaller down payment. This allows investors to control more assets with less of their own money.

There are two main types of leverage in real estate investing:

1. **Traditional leverage:** This involves using a mortgage to finance a property purchase. For example, an investor might put down a 20% down payment and borrow the remaining 80% from a lender.
2. **Creative financing leverage:** This involves using other types of financing, such as hard money loans, private

lenders, or seller financing, to purchase a property with a smaller down payment.

There are several key benefits to using leverage in real estate investing:

1. Increased returns: Leverage can help investors achieve higher returns on their investments. For example, if an investor purchases a property for $100,000 and makes a 20% down payment, they will have invested $20,000 of their own money. If the property appreciates in value by 10%, the investor will have made a profit of $10,000 on their $20,000 investment, for a return of 50%. However, if the investor had purchased the property with a 10% down payment, they would have only invested $10,000 of their own money. If the property appreciates in value by 10%, the investor will have made a profit of $10,000 on their $10,000 investment, for a return of 100%.

2. Reduced risk: Leverage can also help investors reduce their risk. If an investor purchases a property with all of their own money, they are at risk of losing their entire investment if the property declines in value. However, if an investor uses leverage to purchase a property, they are only at risk of losing their down payment if the property declines in value. This is because the lender will still own the majority of the property.

3. Ability to purchase more properties: Leverage can also allow investors to purchase more properties than they could otherwise afford. For example, if an investor has $100,000 in cash, they could purchase a $100,000 property. However, if they use leverage to purchase a property with a 20% down payment, they could purchase a $500,000 property. This allows investors to grow their portfolios more quickly.

Of course, leverage is also a double-edged sword. If the property declines in value, the investors will lose money more quickly than they would if they had not used leverage. Additionally, leverage can increase the investor's monthly mortgage payments and make them more vulnerable to interest rate fluctuations.

Here are some tips for using leverage to finance your real estate investments:

1. Start small: It is better to start with a smaller investment property and gradually build your portfolio than to go all-in on a single property. This will help you to reduce your risk.

2. Only invest in properties that you can afford: Even if you are using leverage, you should only invest in properties that you can afford to lose. This means making sure that you have a positive cash flow from the property, even if the value of the property declines.

3. Have a plan for dealing with unexpected expenses: Real estate investing can be unpredictable, so it is important to have a plan for dealing with unexpected expenses, such as repairs, vacancies, or interest rate increases.

4. Work with a qualified team: It is important to work with a qualified real estate agent, attorney, and accountant when investing in real estate. They can help you to find the right properties, negotiate contracts, and avoid costly mistakes.

Here are some examples of how real estate investors can use leverage to finance their investments:

1. Fix-and-flip investing: Fix-and-flip investors often use leverage to purchase properties that need repairs or renovations. They then fix up the properties and sell them for a profit.

2. Rental property investing: Rental property investors often use leverage to purchase properties that they can rent out to tenants. The rental income can be used to cover the mortgage payment and other expenses, and the investor can also benefit from the appreciation of the property value over time.

3. Real estate syndications: Real estate syndications are investment vehicles that pool money from multiple investors to purchase real estate properties. This allows investors to invest in larger, more expensive properties than they could afford on their own.

3.3. How to find private lenders

Private lenders are individuals or companies that lend money outside of the traditional banking system. They are often willing to lend to real estate investors who may not qualify for a traditional loan, or who need a loan quickly or with flexible terms.

How to find private lenders

There are several ways to find private lenders, including:

1. Networking: Talk to your friends, family, colleagues, and other real estate investors to see if they know any private lenders. You can also attend real estate investment clubs and meetups to network with other investors and potential lenders.

2. Online directories: There are a number of online directories that list private lenders. Some popular directories include the American Association of Private Lenders (AAPL) and the National Association of Mortgage Brokers (NAMB).

3. Hard money lenders: Hard money lenders are a type of private lender that specializes in short-term loans for real estate investors. Hard money loans are typically secured by the property itself, and they often have higher interest rates than traditional loans.

Once you have found a few potential private lenders, you will need to approach them and present your investment proposal. Your proposal should include information about the property you are interested in buying, your renovation plans, and your financial situation. You should also be prepared to answer any questions the lender may have about your experience and investment strategy.

Here are some tips for finding and working with private lenders:

1. Build relationships: It takes time to build relationships with private lenders. Don't expect to get a loan from a private lender the first time you meet them. Get to know them, learn about their investment criteria, and let them know about your investment goals.

2. Be prepared: When you approach a private lender, be prepared to answer any questions they may have about your investment proposal. This includes having a clear understanding of the property you are interested in buying, your renovation plans, and your financial situation.

3. Be honest: Private lenders want to lend to borrowers who are honest and transparent. Be upfront about your investment experience and financial situation. If you have any credit problems or other financial issues, be sure to disclose them to the lender.

4. Be flexible: Private lenders are often more flexible than traditional banks. They may be willing to lend to borrowers with lower credit scores or higher debt-to-income ratios. They may also be willing to offer shorter loan terms or lower interest rates.

Working with private lenders can be a great way to finance your real estate investments, but it is important to do your research and understand the terms of any loan before you sign an agreement.

3.4. How to use hard money loans

Hard money loans are a type of short-term, asset-based loan that is typically used for real estate investing. Hard money lenders are private individuals or companies that lend money based on the value of the property being purchased, rather than the borrower's credit score. Hard money loans can be a good option for real estate investors who need quick financing for a project, such as a fix-and-flip or a rental property.

How to use hard money loans:

1. Find a hard money lender. There are many hard money lenders out there, but it is important to do your research and find a reputable lender. You can ask for referrals from other real estate investors, or search online for hard money lenders in your area.
2. Get pre-approved. Once you have found a hard money lender, you will need to get pre-approved for a loan. This will give you an idea of how much money you can borrow and what your interest rate will be.
3. Find a property. Once you have been pre-approved for a loan, you can start looking for a property to purchase. Keep in mind that hard money lenders typically only

lend on properties that are in good condition and have a clear title.

4. Make an offer. Once you have found a property that you want to purchase, you can make an offer. If your offer is accepted, you will need to sign a purchase contract.
5. Get a hard money loan appraisal. The hard money lender will order an appraisal of the property to determine its value. This will help the lender to determine how much money they are willing to lend.
6. Close on the loan. Once the appraisal has been completed and the loan has been approved, you can close on the loan and purchase the property.

Here are some tips for using hard money loans effectively:

1. Only use hard money loans for short-term projects. Hard money loans typically have high-interest rates, so it is important to use them only for short-term projects, such as fix-and-flip or rental properties.
2. Have a clear plan for how you will repay the loan. Before you take out a hard money loan, make sure that you have a clear plan for how you will repay the loan. This may involve selling the property after you have renovated it, or refinancing the loan with a traditional mortgage.
3. Be aware of the fees associated with hard money loans. Hard money loans typically have high-interest rates and fees. Make sure that you understand all of the fees associated with the loan before you sign any paperwork.

Pros of using hard money loans:

1. Quick financing. Hard money lenders can typically provide financing within a few days or weeks, which is much faster than traditional banks.
2. Flexible terms. Hard money lenders are often willing to work with borrowers with bad credit or who need to finance non-traditional properties.
3. No prepayment penalty. Many hard money lenders do not charge a prepayment penalty, which means that borrowers can pay off their loans early without any additional fees.

Cons of using hard money loans:

1. High interest rates. Hard money loans typically have high interest rates, which can make them expensive.
2. Short repayment terms. Hard money loans typically have short repayment terms, which can make them difficult to repay if the borrower does not have a clear plan in place.
3. High fees. Hard money loans typically have high fees, which can add to the cost of the loan.

Chapter 4: Investing in Fix-and-Flip Properties

4.1. What is fix-and-flip investing?

Fix-and-flip investing is a real estate investment strategy that involves purchasing properties in need of repair or renovation, making the necessary improvements, and then selling the properties at a higher price to generate a profit.

Fix-and-flip investors typically focus on finding properties that are undervalued, either due to their condition or location. Once they have found a property, they will estimate the cost of repairs and renovations, and then factor that into their purchase offer.

Once the property has been purchased, the investor will begin making the necessary repairs and renovations. This can range from simple cosmetic updates to major structural repairs. The goal is to improve the property's condition and appeal to potential buyers.

Once the renovations are complete, the investor will put the property on the market for sale. The goal is to sell the property quickly and for a profit. Fix-and-flip investors typically aim to generate a profit of 20-30% on their investments.

Benefits of fix-and-flip investing

Fix-and-flip investing can be a very lucrative way to make money in real estate. However, it is important to note that it is also a risky investment strategy. There are a number of things that can go wrong, such as unexpected repair costs, market downturns, and difficulty finding buyers.

Despite the risks, there are a number of benefits to fix-and-flip investing, including:

1. The potential for high returns. Fix-and-flip investors can generate profits of 20-30% on their investments, which is much higher than the average return on other types of investments, such as stocks and bonds.
2. The ability to control your own time and income. Fix-and-flip investors are their own bosses, and they can choose how many projects they want to work on at a time. This can be a great way to achieve financial independence.
3. The opportunity to be creative and hands-on. Fix-and-flip investors can use their creativity and skills to transform properties from fixer-uppers to dream homes. This can be a very rewarding experience.

Risks of fix-and-flip investing

While there are a number of benefits to fix-and-flip investing, there are also a number of risks, including:

1. Unexpected repair costs. It is important to have a thorough inspection of any property you are considering purchasing before you make an offer. This will help to identify any potential problems that need to be repaired. However, there is always the possibility of unexpected repair costs arising during the renovation process.
2. Market downturns. The real estate market can be cyclical, and there is always the possibility of a market downturn. If the market downturns while you are working on a fix-and-flip project, it could be difficult to sell the property for a profit.

3. Difficulty finding buyers. Even if the real estate market is strong, there is always the possibility of difficulty finding buyers for your fix-and-flip property. This can be especially true if the property is in a less desirable location or if the renovations are not completed to a high standard.

How to get started with fix-and-flip investing

If you are interested in getting started with fix-and-flip investing, there are a few things you need to do:

1. Educate yourself. There are a number of books, courses, and online resources that can teach you about fix-and-flip investing. It is important to learn as much as you can about the process before you get started.
2. Build a team. You will need a team of professionals to help you with your fix-and-flip projects, including a real estate agent, contractor, and attorney.
3. Secure financing. There are a number of different ways to finance your fix-and-flip projects. You may be able to use your own savings, or you may need to obtain a loan from a bank or lender.
4. Find properties. Once you have a team and financing in place, you can start looking for properties to flip. There are a number of different ways to find properties, such as online real estate listings, auctions, and foreclosures.
5. Renovate the properties. Once you have found a property to flip, you will need to renovate it. This may involve making cosmetic updates, major structural repairs, or both.
6. Sell the properties. Once the renovations are complete, you can put the property on the market for sale. The goal is to sell the property quickly and for a profit.

4.2. How to find fix-and-flip properties

Fix-and-flip properties are properties that are bought for below market value, renovated, and then sold for a profit. This can be a great way to make money in real estate, but it's important to know where to find good deals.

Here are a few tips on how to find fix-and-flip properties:

1. Network with real estate agents. Real estate agents have access to a wide range of properties, including many that are not listed on the market. Let your real estate agent know that you're interested in fix-and-flip properties, and they can help you find good deals.
2. Attend real estate auctions and foreclosure sales. Fix-and-flip properties can often be found at auctions and foreclosure sales. However, it's important to do your research before bidding on a property at auction. Make sure you know the property's value and the estimated cost of repairs.
3. Look for distressed properties. Distressed properties are properties that are in need of repairs or renovations. These properties can often be purchased at a discount, but it's important to factor in the cost of repairs when calculating your potential profit.
4. Use real estate investment software. There are a number of real estate investment software programs that can help you find fix-and-flip properties. These programs can search for properties based on a variety of criteria, such as price, location, and condition.

Once you've found a few potential fix-and-flip properties, it's important to assess each property carefully. Consider the following factors:

- The property's condition. How much work does the property need? What are the estimated costs of repairs?
- The property's location. Is the property in a desirable location? Are there other fix-and-flip properties in the area?
- The property's value. What is the property's after-repair value (ARV)? How much profit can you expect to make?

It's also important to have a realistic understanding of the time and effort required to fix and flip a property. Renovations can take longer than expected, and it can be difficult to find the right buyers. If you're not prepared for the challenges of fix-and-flip investing, it's best to find another investment strategy.

Here are a few additional tips for finding fix-and-flip properties:

1. Drive around your desired neighborhoods. Look for properties that are in need of repairs or renovations. You can also look for properties that are vacant or have liens against them.
2. Check the local classified ads. Fix-and-flip properties are often advertised in the classified ads of local newspapers and magazines.
3. Talk to your friends, family, and colleagues. Let them know that you're interested in fix-and-flip properties. They may be able to lead you to some good deals.
4. Finding fix-and-flip properties can take some time and effort, but it's worth it in the end. By following the tips

above, you can increase your chances of finding good deals and making a profit on your investments.

4.3. How to estimate the cost of repairs and renovations

Estimating the cost of repairs and renovations is an important skill for any real estate investor. It is also important for homeowners who are considering making improvements to their homes. By accurately estimating the cost of a project, you can avoid overspending and make sure that you have enough money to complete the work.

There are a few different ways to estimate the cost of repairs and renovations. One way is to use a cost estimator tool. There are a number of these tools available online and in home improvement stores. Cost estimator tools typically ask you to input information about the project, such as the square footage of the area being renovated, the type of materials being used, and the labor involved. Once you have input all of the information, the tool will generate an estimate of the total cost of the project.

Another way to estimate the cost of repairs and renovations is to get quotes from multiple contractors. This is the most accurate way to estimate the cost of a project, but it can also be the most time-consuming. When getting quotes from contractors, be sure to provide them with as much information as possible about the project. This will help them to give you an accurate estimate.

Once you have a few estimates from contractors, you can compare them to see which one is the best fit for your budget. You should also consider the contractor's experience and reputation when making your decision.

Here are some tips for estimating the cost of repairs and renovations:

1. Be as specific as possible. The more specific you can be about the project, the more accurate your estimate will be. For example, instead of saying "I need to renovate my kitchen," try to be more specific about the type of work that needs to be done, such as "I need to replace the cabinets, countertops, and appliances."

2. Get multiple estimates. As mentioned above, getting multiple estimates from contractors is the most accurate way to estimate the cost of a project.

3. Factor in unexpected costs. When estimating the cost of a project, it is important to factor in unexpected costs. Unexpected costs can include things like finding hidden damage or having to purchase additional materials. It is a good idea to add a 10-20% contingency fund to your estimate to cover unexpected costs.

4. Be flexible with your budget. Once you have an estimate of the cost of the project, you can start to develop a budget. However, it is important to be flexible with your budget. There may be some things that you have to cut back on if the project ends up costing more than you expected.

5. Estimating the cost of repairs and renovations can be a challenging task, but it is an important one. By following the

tips above, you can get an accurate estimate of the cost of your project and avoid overspending.

Here are some additional tips for estimating the cost of specific types of repairs and renovations:

1. Kitchen renovation: The cost of a kitchen renovation can vary widely depending on the size of the kitchen, the type of materials being used, and the scope of the project. However, as a general rule of thumb, you can expect to pay between $10,000 and $45,000 for a kitchen renovation.

2. Bathroom renovation: The cost of a bathroom renovation can also vary depending on the size of the bathroom, the type of materials being used, and the scope of the project. However, as a general rule of thumb, you can expect to pay between $5,000 and $25,000 for a bathroom renovation.

3. Roof replacement: The cost of a roof replacement will depend on the size of the roof, the type of roofing material being used, and the complexity of the job. However, as a general rule of thumb, you can expect to pay between $5,000 and $15,000 for a roof replacement.

4. HVAC replacement: The cost of an HVAC replacement will depend on the size of your home, the type of HVAC system you choose, and the complexity of the installation. However, as a general rule of thumb, you can expect to pay between $5,000 and $10,000 for an HVAC replacement.

Here are some examples of common repairs and renovations and their estimated costs:

- Kitchen renovation: $10,000-$45,000
- Bathroom renovation: $5,000-$25,000
- Roofing replacement: $5,000-$15,000

- Siding replacement: $8,000-$20,000
- Window replacement: $2,000-$8,000 per window
- HVAC replacement: $5,000-$10,000
- Water heater replacement: $1,000-$3,000
- Appliance replacement: $300-$1,500 per appliance
- Flooring replacement: $3-$10 per square foot
- Painting: $2-$5 per square foot
- Drywall repair: $1-$3 per square foot
- Electrical work: $50-$100 per hour
- Plumbing work: $75-$150 per hour

It is important to note that these are just estimates. The actual cost of repairs and renovations will vary depending on the specific project and the location.

If you are unsure about how to estimate the cost of repairs and renovations, it is a good idea to consult with a real estate professional or a contractor. They can help you assess the scope of work and provide you with accurate estimates.

4.4. How to sell your fix-and-flip property for a profit

To sell your fix-and-flip property for a profit, you need to:

1. Price the property correctly. This is perhaps the most important factor in selling your property for a profit. You need to price the property high enough to cover your costs and make a profit, but not so high that it scares away potential buyers. To determine the right price, you should do a comparative market analysis (CMA) to see what similar properties in your area have recently sold for.

2. Make the property appealing to buyers. This means making any necessary repairs and renovations and staging the

property to make it look its best. You should also focus on highlighting the features of the property that are most likely to appeal to buyers in your target market. For example, if you are targeting first-time homebuyers, you might want to highlight the property's convenient location or low-maintenance exterior.

3. Market the property effectively. Once your property is ready to sell, you need to market it to potential buyers. This can be done through a variety of channels, such as online listings, print advertising, and open houses. You should also consider working with a real estate agent who specializes in selling fix-and-flip properties.

Here are some additional tips for selling your fix-and-flip property for a profit:

- Be flexible with your closing date. This will make your property more attractive to buyers who may be on a tight timeline.
- Offer to pay buyer's closing costs. This can help to make your property more affordable for buyers and make it more likely that they will put in an offer.
- Consider selling to a cash buyer. Cash buyers can often close on a property more quickly than buyers who are financing their purchase, which can be beneficial if you are in a hurry to sell.

Here are some common mistakes to avoid when selling your fix-and-flip property:

1. Overpricing the property. This will make it more difficult to sell the property and may lead you to have to reduce the price later on, which can eat into your profits.

2. Not making the necessary repairs and renovations. Buyers will be less likely to make an offer on a property that needs a lot of work.
3. Not staging the property properly. A well-staged property is more likely to make a good impression on potential buyers and encourage them to make an offer.
4. Not marketing the property effectively. If you don't market your property properly, potential buyers won't know about it and you'll be less likely to get offers.

By following these tips, you can increase your chances of selling your fix-and-flip property for a profit.

Chapter 5: Investing in Rental Properties

5.1. What is rental property investing?

Rental property investing is the purchase of real estate to generate income by renting it out to tenants. It can be a great way to build wealth over time, as well as to generate passive income.

When you invest in a rental property, you are essentially becoming a landlord. You will be responsible for purchasing the property, maintaining it, and finding tenants who will pay you rent every month. After paying all of your expenses, such as mortgage payments, property taxes, and insurance, the remaining income is your profit. However, it is important to understand the risks and rewards involved before investing in rental property.

One of the biggest benefits of rental property investing is the potential for high returns. Over the long term, real estate has historically outperformed other asset classes, such as stocks and bonds. This is because real estate is a tangible asset that has a limited supply and a growing demand.

Another benefit of rental property investing is that it can provide a steady stream of income. Once you have purchased a rental property and found tenants, you can expect to receive rent payments regularly. This can be a great way to supplement your regular income or to provide a retirement paycheck.

However, there are also some risks associated with rental property investing. One of the biggest risks is the potential for vacancy. If you are unable to find tenants for your property, you will not be generating any income. Additionally, you will still be responsible for the mortgage payments, property taxes, and other expenses.

Another risk associated with rental property investing is the potential for damage to the property. Tenants may accidentally or deliberately damage your property, which could result in costly repairs. Additionally, you may be responsible for the cost of repairs to the property if they are caused by natural disasters, such as a fire or flood.

Despite the risks, rental property investing can be a great way to build wealth and generate passive income. However, it is important to do your research and understand the risks involved before investing.

Here are some tips for successful rental property investing:

1. Do your research. Before you buy any rental property, it is important to research the local real estate market and the specific property you are considering. This will help you to determine if the property is a good investment and what you can expect to earn in rent.
2. Find the right property. Not all rental properties are created equal. When choosing a rental property, you should consider factors such as the location, the condition of the property, and the potential for rent growth.
3. Screen your tenants carefully. Once you have found a rental property, you will need to screen potential tenants carefully. This will help you avoid renting to tenants who are likely to damage your property or not pay their rent.
4. Manage your property effectively. Once you have tenants in place, you will need to manage your property

effectively. This includes collecting rent, handling maintenance issues, and dealing with tenant complaints.

5. Be prepared for unexpected expenses. Even the best-managed rental properties can have unexpected expenses, such as repairs or vacancies. It is important to have a financial cushion in place to cover these unexpected expenses.

If you are considering investing in rental property, it is important to weigh the risks and rewards carefully. Rental property investing can be a great way to build wealth and generate passive income, but it is important to do your research and be prepared for the unexpected.

5.2. How to find rental properties

Finding rental properties can be a challenge, especially in competitive markets. However, there are several things you can do to increase your chances of finding a good property to rent out.

1. Know what you're looking for

Before you start your search, it's important to have a clear idea of what you're looking for in a rental property. This includes things like:

a. Location: Where do you want your rental property to be located? Consider factors such as proximity to schools, jobs, and amenities.

b. Property type: What type of property are you looking for? Do you want to rent out a single-family home, a condo, or an apartment?

c. Size: How many bedrooms and bathrooms do you need?

d. Amenities: What amenities are important to you? Some common amenities include things like a garage, washer and dryer hookups, and a backyard.

e. Budget: How much can you afford to spend on a rental property?

2. Use rental listing websites

One of the best ways to find rental properties is to use rental listing websites. There are several different websites to choose from, such as:

- Zillow
- Trulia
- Apartments.com
- Rent.com
- Craigslist

These websites allow you to search for rental properties based on your criteria, such as location, property type, size, and amenities.

3. Network with other real estate investors

Another great way to find rental properties is to network with other real estate investors. You can do this by attending real estate meetups and conferences, or by joining online real estate investing forums.

Other real estate investors may have rental properties that they're looking to sell, or they may know of other investors who are looking to rent out their properties.

4. Work with a real estate agent

If you're serious about finding a rental property, you may want to consider working with a real estate agent. Real estate agents have access to a network of listings that you may not be able to find on your own. They can also help you negotiate the lease agreement and ensure that you're getting a good deal.

Once you've found a few potential rental properties, it's important to do your research before making a decision. This includes things like:

- Checking the crime rate in the neighborhood
- Researching the school district
- Reading reviews of the property management company
- Getting a home inspection

By doing your research, you can increase your chances of finding a good rental property that will be a profitable investment.

Here are some questions to ask yourself when evaluating a potential rental property:

- Is the property in a good location?
- Is the property in good condition?
- Are there any major repairs or renovations that need to be done?
- What are the terms of the lease agreement?
- What are the monthly rent and security deposit?
- Who is responsible for utilities and maintenance?

Once you have found a rental property that you are interested in, you should schedule a time to view the property with the landlord or property manager. This will give you a chance to see the property in person and ask any questions that you have.

If you are happy with the property, you can then negotiate the lease agreement and sign a lease. Be sure to read the lease agreement carefully before signing it, and make sure that you understand all of the terms and conditions.

Finding the right rental property can take some time and effort, but it is worth it to find a property that is in a good location, in good condition, and affordable.

5.3. How to screen tenants

Screening tenants is one of the most important steps in the real estate investing process. By carefully screening tenants, you can reduce your risk of evictions, rent defaults, and property damage.

There are several different steps you can take to screen tenants, including:

1. Require a rental application. The rental application should include basic information about the applicant, such as their name, contact information, employment history, and rental history. You should also ask for references, such as previous landlords and employers.

2. Run a credit report and background check. A credit report will give you an idea of the applicant's financial history, including their payment history and debt levels. A background check will reveal any criminal records or evictions.

3. Verify income and employment. You should ask to see proof of income, such as pay stubs or bank statements. You should also contact the applicant's employer to verify their employment and salary.

4. Check previous addresses, landlords, and eviction history. You should contact the applicant's previous landlords to get

their feedback on the applicant's rental history. You should also check the applicant's eviction history to see if they have been evicted from any previous rentals.

5. Interview applicants and ask screening questions. When you interview applicants, you should ask them questions about their rental history, their reasons for moving, and their plans for the future. You should also ask them questions about their lifestyle and habits, such as whether they have pets or smoke.

Here are some specific screening questions you can ask tenants:

- Why are you moving?
- How long have you lived at your current residence?
- What was your monthly rent?
- Have you ever been evicted?
- Do you have any pets?
- Do you smoke?
- What is your employment status?
- What is your monthly income?
- What is your credit score?

It is important to note that you cannot discriminate against tenants on the basis of race, religion, national origin, sex, family status, or disability. You should also avoid asking tenants about their personal beliefs or political affiliations.

Once you have screened all of your applicants, you can select the tenant who you believe is the best fit for your property and who you believe will be a responsible and reliable tenant.

Here are some additional tips for screening tenants:

- Be consistent with your screening criteria. Don't make exceptions for one applicant that you wouldn't make for another.
- Trust your gut instinct. If you have a bad feeling about an applicant, don't rent to them.
- Get everything in writing. Once you have selected a tenant, be sure to put their lease agreement in writing. This will help to protect you in case of any problems down the road.
- By carefully screening tenants, you can reduce your risk of problems and protect your investment.

5.4. How to manage your rental properties

Managing rental properties can be a complex and time-consuming task, but it is essential to do so effectively in order to maximize your profits and minimize your stress. Here are some tips on how to manage your rental properties effectively:

1. Screen tenants carefully.

One of the most important things you can do to protect your investment is to screen tenants carefully. This means checking their credit history, employment history, and rental references. You should also interview potential tenants and get to know them personally. This will help you to choose tenants who are likely to pay their rent on time and take care of your property.

2. Set clear expectations.

Once you have selected tenants, it is important to set clear expectations for them. This includes providing them with a copy of the lease agreement and reviewing it with them line by line. You should also discuss your expectations for things like rent payments, maintenance requests, and noise levels.

3. Be responsive to maintenance requests.

When your tenants have maintenance requests, it is important to be responsive and address them promptly. This shows your tenants that you care about their well-being and that you are committed to maintaining your property in good condition. It is also important to keep records of all maintenance requests and the work that was done to address them.

4. Enforce the lease agreement.

If your tenants violate the terms of the lease agreement, it is important to enforce the agreement fairly and consistently. This may involve issuing a warning letter, charging a late fee, or even evicting the tenants. It is important to remember that the lease agreement is a legally binding contract, and you have the right to enforce its terms.

5. Hire a property manager.

If you do not have the time or energy to manage your rental properties yourself, you may want to consider hiring a property manager. Property managers can take care of all of the day-to-day tasks involved in managing rental properties, such as screening tenants, collecting rent, and handling maintenance requests.

Here are some additional tips for managing your rental properties effectively:

1. Document everything. Keep detailed records of all of your interactions with your tenants, including rent payments, maintenance requests, and lease violations. This will help to protect you in the event of a legal dispute.

2. Stay organized. Keep all of your rental property paperwork organized in a file cabinet or electronic file system. This will

make it easy to find the information you need when you need it.

3. Be proactive. Don't wait for your tenants to come to you with problems. Be proactive and inspect your properties regularly to identify any potential problems early on.

4. Network with other landlords. There are many online and offline communities where landlords can connect and share tips on how to manage their properties effectively.

Managing rental properties can be a challenging task, but it is important to remember that it is also an opportunity to generate passive income and build wealth over time. By following the tips above, you can manage your rental properties effectively and maximize your profits.

Chapter 6: Investing in Real Estate Syndications

6.1. What is a real estate syndication?

A real estate syndication is a partnership between a group of investors who pool their resources together to purchase a real estate property or portfolio of properties. The syndication is typically managed by a sponsor, who is responsible for finding the investment opportunities, underwriting the deals, and overseeing the management of the properties. Investors in the syndication are passive investors, meaning that they do not have any direct involvement in the day-to-day management of the properties.

Real estate syndications can be structured in a number of different ways, but the most common type is a limited partnership (LP). In an LP, the sponsor is the general partner and the investors are the limited partners. The general partner is responsible for managing the partnership and making all of the investment decisions. The limited partners are passive investors and have limited liability, meaning that they are only liable for their investment amount.

Real estate syndications offer a number of advantages for investors, including:

1. Access to larger and more complex real estate deals that would not be possible for individual investors to purchase on their own.
2. Diversification: Investors can spread their risk across multiple properties and asset classes.
3. Professional management: The syndication is managed by a sponsor who has the experience and expertise to manage the properties effectively.

4. Passive income: Investors can earn passive income from the cash flow generated by the properties.

However, there are also some risks associated with real estate syndications, including:

1. Illiquidity: Real estate investments are typically illiquid, meaning that they can be difficult to sell quickly.
2. Lack of control: Investors have limited control over the investment decisions made by the sponsor.
3. Fraud: There is always the risk of fraud in any type of investment, but it is particularly important to be vigilant when investing in real estate syndications.

How to invest in a real estate syndication

If you are interested in investing in a real estate syndication, there are a few things you should do:

1. Do your research: Before you invest in any syndication, it is important to do your research on the sponsor and the investment opportunity. Make sure that the sponsor has a good track record and that the investment opportunity makes sense for you.

2. Read the offering documents carefully: Once you have found a syndication that you are interested in, it is important to read the offering documents carefully. These documents will outline all of the risks and potential rewards of the investment.

3. Ask questions: If you have any questions about the syndication, do not hesitate to ask the sponsor. They should be able to answer all of your questions thoroughly and honestly.

Real estate syndications can be a great way for investors to invest in real estate on a budget and gain access to larger and more complex deals. However, it is important to do your research and understand the risks involved before investing in any syndication.

Here are some additional things to consider when investing in a real estate syndication:

1. Fees: Syndicators typically charge a number of fees, including an acquisition fee, a management fee, and a performance fee. It is important to understand these fees and how they will impact your returns.

2. Investment horizon: Real estate syndications are typically long-term investments. It is important to be patient and understand that you may not be able to access your capital quickly.

3. Minimum investment: Syndications typically have a minimum investment requirement. This amount can vary depending on the syndication, but it is typically between $10,000 and $50,000.

6.2. How to find real estate syndications

Real estate syndications are a great way to invest in real estate passively, without having to manage the properties yourself. However, because syndications are private investments, they can be difficult to find. Here are a few tips on how to find real estate syndications:

1. Network with other real estate investors. One of the best ways to find syndications is to network with other real estate investors. Attend real estate meetups, conferences, and events. Join online real estate investment forums and groups. Talk to your friends, family, and colleagues who invest in real estate.

2. Use real estate syndication platforms. There are a number of real estate syndication platforms that connect investors with

syndicators. These platforms typically require investors to be accredited. Some popular real estate syndication platforms include:

- CrowdStreet
- RealtyMogul
- PeerStreet
- AcreTrader
- Fundrise

3. Search online. You can also search online for real estate syndications. There are a number of websites and blogs that list syndication opportunities. Some popular websites include:

- Real Estate Crowdfunding Review
- Passive Income Investing
- The Real Estate Syndication Podcast
- The Real Estate Investing Mastery Podcast

4. Work with a real estate investment advisor. A real estate investment advisor can help you find syndications that meet your investment goals and risk tolerance. They can also help you evaluate syndications and make informed investment decisions.

Once you have found a few syndications that you are interested in, it is important to do your research. Evaluate the syndicator's track record, investment strategy, and fees. Read the private placement memorandum (PPM) carefully. Ask questions and get everything in writing.

Tips for evaluating real estate syndications

When evaluating real estate syndications, consider the following factors:

1. Syndicator's track record. How many syndications has the syndicator completed? What is their success rate?
2. Investment strategy. What type of real estate does the syndicator invest in? What is their investment strategy?
3. Fees. What are the syndicator's fees? Are they reasonable?
4. Property. What type of property is the syndication investing in? Is it in a good location? Is it in good condition?
5. Exit strategy. What is the syndicator's exit strategy? How do they plan to sell the property and return profits to investors?

It is also important to understand the risks associated with real estate syndications. Real estate syndications are illiquid investments, meaning that you cannot easily cash out your investment. There is also the risk of losing money if the syndicator makes bad investment decisions or if the property market declines.

6.3. How to evaluate real estate syndications

Real estate syndications can be a great way to invest in real estate without having to manage the properties yourself. However, it is important to carefully evaluate any syndication opportunity before investing. Here are some key factors to consider:

1. Sponsor

The sponsor of a real estate syndication is arguably the most important factor to consider when evaluating an investment opportunity. The sponsor is responsible for all aspects of the syndication, from finding and underwriting the investment property to managing the property and distributing returns to investors. Therefore, it is crucial to choose a sponsor with a strong track record of success and a proven ability to execute on their business plan.

Here are some key things to look for in a real estate syndication sponsor:

1. Experience and track record: The sponsor should have a deep understanding of the real estate market and a proven track record of success in syndicating and managing real estate investments. Look for sponsors who have a good mix of experience in different asset classes and market cycles.

2. Reputation: The sponsor should have a good reputation in the real estate industry. Ask for references from previous investors and partners. Check to see if the sponsor has any complaints against them with the Better Business Bureau or other regulatory agencies.

3. Alignment of interests: The sponsor should have their interests aligned with those of the investors. Look for sponsors who are investing their own money in the syndication. This demonstrates that they have skin in the game and are committed to the success of the investment.

4. Communication and transparency: The sponsor should be willing to communicate openly and transparently with investors. They should be able to clearly explain the investment opportunity, the risks involved, and their plan for execution.

In addition to the above factors, you should also consider the following when evaluating a real estate syndication sponsor:

1. Investment philosophy and strategy: Does the sponsor's investment philosophy and strategy align with your own? For example, do they focus on value-add investments or core-plus investments? Do they invest in a specific asset class or geographic region?

2. Team: Does the sponsor have a team of experienced and qualified professionals in place? This includes an investment team, asset management team, and accounting team.

3. Fee structure: What fees does the sponsor charge? Are the fees reasonable and transparent?

4. Exit strategy: Does the sponsor have a clear exit strategy for the investment? How and when do they plan to distribute returns to investors?

By carefully evaluating the sponsor, you can increase your chances of success when investing in a real estate syndication.

2. Investment Property

Investment property is one of the most important factors to consider when evaluating a real estate syndication. The type, location, condition, and potential for appreciation of the property will all have a significant impact on the syndication's overall performance.

Type of Property

The type of property that the syndication is investing in will depend on the sponsor's investment strategy. Some of the most common types of investment properties include:

1. **Multifamily:** Multifamily properties, such as apartments and townhouses, can be a good source of recurring income and appreciation potential.
2. **Commercial:** Commercial properties, such as office buildings and retail centers, can also be a good source of

income, but they may be more volatile than multifamily properties.

3. **Industrial:** Industrial properties, such as warehouses and manufacturing facilities, can be a good investment for investors who are looking for long-term income and appreciation.

4. **Land:** Land can be a good investment for investors who are looking for long-term appreciation potential. However, it is important to do your research and make sure that the land is in a desirable location and has the potential to be developed in the future.

Location

The location of the investment property is also very important. Properties in desirable locations are more likely to appreciate in value and command higher rents. When evaluating a syndication, consider the following factors:

1. **Job market:** A strong job market is a good indicator of future demand for housing and commercial space.

2. **Population growth:** Areas with strong population growth tend to have higher demand for housing and commercial space.

3. **Crime rate:** A low crime rate is important for both residential and commercial properties.

4. **Schools:** Good schools are important for families, which can make residential properties more attractive to tenants.

5. **Amenities:** Close proximity to amenities, such as shopping, dining, and entertainment, can make both residential and commercial properties more attractive.

Condition of the Property

The condition of the investment property is also important to consider. Properties in good condition are more likely to command higher rents and appreciate in value. When evaluating a syndication, consider the following factors:

1. **Age of the property:** Newer properties are generally in better condition than older properties.
2. **Maintenance history:** A well-maintained property is less likely to need major repairs in the near future.
3. **Capital expenditures:** The syndication's PPM should disclose any upcoming capital expenditures that will be required for the property.

Potential for Appreciation

The potential for appreciation is another important factor to consider when evaluating a real estate syndication. Properties in desirable locations and with strong fundamentals are more likely to appreciate in value. When evaluating a syndication, consider the following factors:

1. **Market trends:** Are property values in the area trending up or down?
2. **Development potential:** Is the property located in an area that is likely to be developed in the future?
3. **Zoning:** Is the property zoned for the intended use?

By carefully considering all of the factors above, you can make an informed decision about whether or not to invest in a real estate syndication.

3. Deal Structure

The deal structure of a real estate syndication is one of the most important factors to consider when evaluating an investment opportunity. The deal structure outlines the rights, responsibilities, and financial arrangements between the sponsor and investors.

There are many different ways to structure a real estate syndication. However, some of the most common deal structures include:

1. **Straight split:** The sponsor and investors share the profits and losses of the syndication in a predetermined ratio. For example, the sponsor may receive 20% of the profits and the investors may receive 80% of the profits.
2. **Waterfall:** The waterfall structure is more complex than a straight split. It typically involves a preferred return for investors, followed by a performance-based fee for the sponsor. For example, investors may receive a 6% preferred return on their investment, followed by a 20% share of the profits above the preferred return.
3. **Hybrid:** A hybrid deal structure combines elements of a straight split and a waterfall. For example, investors may receive a 70% share of the profits up to a certain point, followed by a 50/50 split of the profits above that point.

In addition to the split of profits and losses, the deal structure will also typically address the following:

1. **Investment terms:** The investment terms will outline the minimum investment amount, holding period, and other important details.
2. **Fees:** The sponsor will typically charge a variety of fees, such as an acquisition fee, management fee, and performance fee.

3. **Distribution waterfall:** The distribution waterfall will outline how profits and losses will be distributed to the sponsor and investors.

It is important to carefully review the deal structure of any real estate syndication before investing. You should make sure that you understand the rights and responsibilities of all parties involved, and that the deal structure is aligned with your investment goals and risk tolerance.

Here are some additional things to consider when evaluating the deal structure of a real estate syndication:

- **Sponsor alignment:** The deal structure should be aligned with the sponsor's interests. For example, if the sponsor is incentivized to sell the property quickly, the distribution waterfall may favor them over investors.
- **Investor liquidity:** The deal structure should allow investors to exit the investment if they need to. For example, the syndication may offer buybacks or other liquidity options.
- **Tax implications:** The deal structure should be designed to minimize the tax liability of all parties involved.
- **Transparency:** The deal structure should be transparent and easy to understand. Investors should be able to see how their investment will be used and how profits and losses will be distributed.

4. Projected Returns

Projected returns are one of the most important factors to consider when evaluating a real estate syndication. Syndication sponsors will typically provide investors with projected returns, but it is important to keep in mind that these projections are just estimates and past performance is not indicative of future results.

Syndication sponsors use a variety of methods to project returns, including:

1. **Income and expense projections:** This method involves estimating the rental income and operating expenses of the investment property over the hold period. The sponsor will then use these projections to calculate the net operating income (NOI) and cash flow.
2. **Comparable sales:** This method involves comparing the investment property to similar properties that have recently sold. The sponsor will then use this information to estimate the value of the investment property at the end of the hold period.
3. **Discounted cash flow (DCF) analysis:** This method involves discounting the future cash flows of the investment property to arrive at a present value. The DCF analysis takes into account the time value of money and the risks associated with the investment.

Once the sponsor has projected the returns for the investment property, they will develop a distribution waterfall. The distribution waterfall outlines how the investment proceeds will be distributed to investors. The distribution waterfall will typically include a preferred return for the sponsor, followed by a return to investors.

When evaluating the projected returns of a real estate syndication, it is important to consider the following factors:

1. **The sponsor's track record:** Syndication sponsors with a proven track record of success are more likely to achieve their projected returns.
2. **The investment property:** The type, location, and condition of the investment property will all impact its potential for appreciation and cash flow.
3. **The deal structure:** The deal structure, including the investment terms, fees, and distribution waterfall, will also impact the projected returns.
4. **The market:** The overall real estate market will also impact the projected returns.

It is also important to remember that real estate syndications are illiquid investments. This means that it can be difficult to sell your investment interest if you need to access your capital.

Overall, projected returns are an important factor to consider when evaluating a real estate syndication. However, it is important to keep in mind that these projections are just estimates and there is always the risk of losing money.

Here are some additional tips for evaluating the projected returns of a real estate syndication:

- Ask the sponsor to explain their methodology for projecting returns.
- Get the projected returns in writing.
- Have a qualified financial advisor review the projected returns.
- Compare the projected returns to other investment opportunities.

5. Due Diligence

Due diligence is the process of investigating a potential investment to assess its risks and potential rewards. It is an essential step in any investment process, but it is especially important when evaluating real estate syndications.

Here are some of the key areas to focus on when conducting due diligence on a real estate syndication:

1. **Sponsor:** The sponsor is the person or company that is responsible for managing the syndication and its investments. It is important to research the sponsor's experience, track record, and reputation. You should also make sure that the sponsor's investment goals and risk tolerance are aligned with your own.

2. **Investment property:** Evaluate the investment property itself, including its type, location, condition, and potential for appreciation. You should also understand the property's operating expenses and potential rental income.

3. **Deal structure:** Real estate syndications can have different deal structures. It is important to understand how the syndication is structured, including the investment terms, fees, and distribution waterfall. You should also make sure that you understand your rights and responsibilities as an investor.

4. **Financial projections:** Syndication sponsors will typically provide investors with projected returns. However, it is important to keep in mind that these projections are just estimates and past performance is not indicative of future results. You should carefully review the syndication's financial projections and make

your own assessment of the risks and potential rewards.

5. **Legal documents:** Review the syndication's PPM (private placement memorandum) and other important legal documents. This will help you to understand the terms of the investment and your rights and obligations as an investor.

In addition to the above, you may also want to consider the following when conducting due diligence on a real estate syndication:

1. **Speak with other investors:** If you can, speak with other investors who have invested in syndications managed by the same sponsor. This can give you valuable insights into the sponsor's performance and the investment process.

2. **Get everything in writing:** Make sure that all of the terms of the investment are in writing, including the investment terms, fees, and distribution waterfall. This will help to protect your interests in the event of any disputes.

Due diligence can be a time-consuming process, but it is essential for making informed investment decisions. By carefully evaluating a real estate syndication before investing, you can reduce your risk of loss and increase your chances of success.

6.4. How to invest in real estate syndications

To invest in a real estate syndication, you will typically need to be an accredited investor. This means that you must have an annual income of at least $200,000 ($300,000 for a married couple) or a net worth of at least $1 million, excluding your primary residence.

Once you have confirmed that you are an accredited investor, you can start looking for real estate syndication opportunities. There are several ways to do this, including:

- Online real estate crowdfunding platforms
- Real estate investment clubs
- Networking with other real estate investors
- Attending real estate investment conferences

Once you have found a syndication opportunity that you are interested in, you will need to review the private placement memorandum (PPM). This document will provide you with all of the important information about the syndication, including the investment terms, fees, and risks.

Once you have reviewed the PPM and are comfortable with the investment, you can sign the subscription agreement and send in your investment funds.

Here is a more detailed overview of the steps involved in investing in a real estate syndication:

- Find a real estate syndication opportunity. There are a number of ways to do this, as mentioned above.
- Review the private placement memorandum (PPM). The PPM will provide you with all of the important information about the syndication, including the investment terms, fees, and risks.
- Decide how much to invest. The minimum investment amount for a real estate syndication can vary from deal to deal. However, it is typically at least $25,000.

- Sign the subscription agreement and send in your investment funds. Once you have signed the subscription agreement, you will need to send in your investment funds to the syndication sponsor.

Once you have invested in a real estate syndication, the sponsor will be responsible for managing the investment property on your behalf. You will receive periodic updates from the sponsor on the performance of the investment.

Here are some additional tips for investing in real estate syndications:

1. Do your research. Before investing in any real estate syndication, it is important to do your research on the sponsor, the investment property, and the deal structure.
2. Invest for the long term. Real estate syndications are typically long-term investments. You should expect to hold your investment for at least 5-7 years.
3. Diversify your portfolio. Don't put all of your eggs in one basket. Consider investing in multiple real estate syndications to diversify your risk.

Chapter 7: Investing in REITs

7.1. What are REITs?

REITs, or real estate investment trusts, are companies that own, operate, or finance income-producing real estate. REITs can invest in a variety of property types, including office buildings, shopping malls, apartments, hotels, resorts, self-storage facilities, warehouses, and mortgages or loans.

REITs are traded on major stock exchanges, and they offer a number of benefits to investors, including:

1. **High dividend yields:** REITs are required to distribute at least 90% of their taxable income to shareholders in the form of dividends. This makes REITs a good source of income for investors.
2. **Diversification:** REITs can provide diversification to an investment portfolio. REITs are not correlated to the stock market, and they can provide a hedge against inflation.
3. **Liquidity:** REITs are traded on major stock exchanges, which makes them a liquid investment. Investors can easily buy and sell REIT shares.

REITs are a good investment option for a variety of investors, including retirees, income investors, and investors who are looking to diversify their portfolios.

Types of REITs

There are two main types of REITs: equity REITs and mortgage REITs.

1. **Equity REITs:** Equity REITs own and operate income-producing real estate. Equity REITs generate income from rent and capital appreciation.

2. **Mortgage REITs:** Mortgage REITs invest in real estate mortgages and other real estate-related debt securities. Mortgage REITs generate income from interest payments and premiums on mortgage loans.

How to invest in REITs

Investors can invest in REITs by purchasing shares of individual REITs or by investing in REIT ETFs or mutual funds. REIT ETFs and mutual funds track a basket of REIT stocks, which provides investors with diversification.

REITs invest in a wide variety of real estate property types, including:

- Office buildings
- Apartment buildings
- Shopping centers
- Hotels
- Hospitals
- Warehouses
- Data centers
- Cell towers
- Timberland

Benefits of investing in REITs

REITs offer a number of benefits to investors, including:

1. High dividend yields: REITs are required to distribute at least 90% of their taxable income to shareholders in the form of dividends. This makes REITs a good source of income for investors.

2. Diversification: REITs can provide diversification to an investment portfolio. REITs are not correlated to the stock market, and they can provide a hedge against inflation.

3. Liquidity: REITs are traded on major stock exchanges, which makes them a liquid investment. Investors can easily buy and sell REIT shares.

4. Tax advantages: REITs offer several tax advantages to investors, including the ability to defer capital gains taxes.

Risks of investing in REITs

REITs, like all investments, are subject to risk. Some of the risks associated with investing in REITs include:

1. Interest rate risk: REITs are sensitive to interest rates. Rising interest rates can make it more expensive for REITs to borrow money, which can reduce their profits.

2. Economic risk: REITs are also sensitive to the overall economy. A recession can lead to a decline in demand for commercial real estate, which can reduce REITs' rental income.

3. Property value risk: The value of REITs can also be affected by the value of the properties they own. A decline in property values can lead to a decline in REITs' share prices.

Overall, REITs can be a good investment option for investors who are looking for a high dividend yield, diversification, and liquidity. However, it is important to understand the risks associated with investing in REITs before investing.

REITs are a great way for investors to gain exposure to the real estate market without having to buy, manage, or finance properties themselves. REITs offer several benefits, including high dividend yields, diversification, and liquidity.

7.2. How to invest in REITs

Real Estate Investment Trusts (REITs) are companies that own and operate income-producing real estate. REITs are required by law to pay out at least 90% of their taxable income to shareholders in the form of dividends. This makes REITs a popular investment for income-seeking investors.

There are two main ways to invest in REITs:

1. Directly investing in REIT shares: This involves buying and selling shares of individual REITs on the stock market. There are many different types of REITs available, so you can choose to invest in specific property sectors (e.g., residential, commercial, healthcare, etc.) or in REITs that specialize in different investment strategies (e.g., equity REITs, mortgage REITs, hybrid REITs).

2. Investing in REIT mutual funds or ETFs: REIT mutual funds and ETFs pool money from investors and invest it in a basket of REIT stocks. This can be a good way to get diversified exposure to the REIT market without having to pick individual REIT stocks.

When choosing REITs to invest in, there are a few key factors to consider:

1. **Dividend yield:** REITs are known for their high dividend yields. However, it is important to choose REITs with sustainable dividend yields. REITs that pay out more than 90% of their taxable income in dividends may not be able to maintain their high dividend yields over the long term.
2. **Property type:** REITs invest in a variety of different property types, including residential, commercial, healthcare, industrial, and hospitality. Choose REITs

that invest in the property types that you believe have the most potential for growth and income generation.

3. **Management team:** The management team of a REIT is important to consider, as they are responsible for making investment decisions and managing the REIT's portfolio. Choose REITs with experienced and qualified management teams.

4. **Financial stability:** REITs are required to file financial statements with the Securities and Exchange Commission (SEC). Review the REIT's financial statements to assess its financial stability and performance.

Once you have chosen the REITs that you want to invest in, you can purchase them through a brokerage account. REITs are traded on the stock market, so you can buy and sell them just like any other stock.

Here are some additional tips for investing in REITs:

1. **Reinvest your dividends:** REITs typically pay dividends every quarter. You can reinvest your dividends to buy more shares of the REIT, which can help you to grow your investment over time.

2. **Hold REITs for the long term:** REITs are a long-term investment. The real estate market can be cyclical, so there will be times when REIT prices go down. However, over the long term, REITs have historically outperformed other asset classes, such as bonds and cash.

3. **Diversify your portfolio:** REITs can be a good way to diversify your investment portfolio. However, it is important to invest in other asset classes as well, such

as stocks and bonds. This will help to reduce your overall risk.

7.3. The benefits of investing in REITs

Real Estate Investment Trusts (REITs) offer investors several benefits, including:

1. High dividend yields: REITs are required by law to pay out at least 90% of their taxable income to shareholders in the form of dividends. This makes REITs a popular investment for income-seeking investors. REITs typically have higher dividend yields than other asset classes, such as stocks and bonds.

2. Liquidity: REITs are traded on the stock market, so they can be bought and sold easily. This makes REITs a more liquid investment than direct ownership of real estate.

3. Diversification: REITs can help to diversify an investment portfolio. REITs are not correlated with other asset classes, such as stocks and bonds. This means that REITs can help to reduce overall portfolio risk.

4. Potential for capital appreciation: In addition to income, REITs also offer the potential for capital appreciation. The value of REIT shares can increase over time as the underlying real estate assets appreciate.

5. Inflation protection: Real estate assets tend to appreciate over time, which can help to protect investors from inflation. REITs can provide investors with exposure to real estate without having to directly own or manage real estate assets.

Here are some specific examples of how REITs can benefit investors:

1. Retirement income: REITs can be a good source of income for retirees. REITs offer high dividend yields, which can provide retirees with a steady stream of income.

2. Diversification for younger investors: REITs can also be a good investment for younger investors who are looking to diversify their portfolios. REITs are not correlated with other asset classes, such as stocks and bonds. This means that adding REITs to a portfolio can help to reduce overall portfolio risk.

3. Tax advantages: REITs offer some tax advantages to investors. For example, qualified REIT dividends are taxed as ordinary income, which is typically lower than the tax rate on capital gains.

Overall, REITs can be a good investment for investors of all ages who are looking for income, diversification, and the potential for capital appreciation.

Here are some additional benefits of investing in REITs:

1. REITs can be a good way to invest in specific real estate sectors. For example, investors can invest in REITs that specialize in residential real estate, commercial real estate, healthcare real estate, or industrial real estate. This allows investors to target the specific real estate sectors that they believe have the most potential for growth and income generation.
2. REITs can be a good way to invest in real estate in different geographic locations. For example, investors can invest in REITs that own properties in the United States, Canada, Europe, or Asia. This allows investors to diversify their real estate exposure across different geographic regions.

3. REITs can be a good way to invest in real estate without having to directly own or manage real estate assets. REITs are managed by experienced professionals who have the expertise to identify and invest in high-quality real estate assets.
4. REITs are a relatively low-cost way to invest in real estate. REITs are traded on the stock market, so investors can buy and sell them in small increments. This makes REITs a more affordable investment than direct ownership of real estate.

Overall, REITs offer several benefits to investors, including high dividend yields, liquidity, diversification, potential for capital appreciation, inflation protection, tax advantages, and the ability to invest in specific real estate sectors, geographic locations, and asset classes.

7.4. The risks of investing in REITs

REITs are a popular investment for many investors, but like any investment, they carry risks. Here are some of the key risks to consider before investing in REITs:

1. Interest rate risk: REITs are sensitive to interest rates. When interest rates rise, the value of REITs can fall. This is because REITs typically borrow money to finance their operations and acquisitions. When interest rates rise, the cost of borrowing money increases, which can reduce REITs' profitability.

2. Economic risk: REITs are also sensitive to the overall economy. When the economy is strong, demand for real estate tends to be high. However, when the economy is weak, demand for real estate can decline, which can lead to lower rents and occupancy rates for REITs.

3. Property risk: REITs invest in a variety of different property types. Each property type has its unique risks. For example, residential REITs are exposed to the risk of defaults on mortgages. Commercial REITs are exposed to the risk of tenant bankruptcies.

4. Management risk: The management team of a REIT is responsible for making investment decisions and managing the REIT's portfolio. If the management team is not experienced or qualified, it can lead to poor investment decisions and losses for investors.

5. Liquidity risk: REITs are traded on the stock market, but they can be less liquid than other types of investments, such as stocks and bonds. This means that it may be more difficult to sell REIT shares quickly, especially if the market is volatile.

In addition to these general risks, there are also some specific risks associated with different types of REITs. For example, mortgage REITs are exposed to the risk of prepayments, which can occur when borrowers pay off their mortgages early. Hybrid REITs, which invest in both real estate and mortgages, are exposed to the risks of both asset classes.

It is important to carefully consider the risks associated with REITs before investing. You should also diversify your investment portfolio by investing in other asset classes as well, such as stocks and bonds. This will help to reduce your overall risk.

Here are some tips for mitigating the risks of investing in REITs:

- Invest in a variety of different REITs to diversify your portfolio.

- Invest in REITs with a strong track record and experienced management team.
- Reinvest your dividends to grow your investment over time.
- Have a long-term investment horizon. REITs are a long-term investment, so don't expect to get rich quickly.

By following these tips, you can reduce the risks of investing in REITs and increase your chances of success.

Chapter 8: Real Estate Investing Taxes

8.1. The different types of real estate investment taxes

Real estate investors are subject to a variety of taxes, including income taxes, capital gains taxes, and property taxes.

1. Income taxes

Income taxes are one of the most significant tax considerations for real estate investors. Rental income is taxed as ordinary income, meaning that it is taxed at the investor's regular income tax rate. This can be as high as 37%, depending on the investor's income level.

However, there are several deductions that real estate investors can take to reduce their taxable income, including:

1. **Mortgage interest:** Real estate investors can deduct the interest that they pay on their mortgages. This can be a significant deduction, especially for investors who have recently purchased properties with large mortgages.
2. **Property taxes:** Real estate investors can also deduct the property taxes that they pay on their investment properties.
3. **Depreciation:** Depreciation is a non-cash expense that allows real estate investors to deduct the cost of their investment properties over time. This can be a significant deduction for investors who own long-term rental properties.
4. **Other expenses:** Real estate investors can also deduct other expenses related to their investment properties, such as repairs and maintenance, insurance, and management fees.

It is important to note that real estate investors are only able to deduct expenses that are incurred in the course of their business. This means that personal expenses, such as travel expenses to visit vacation rental properties, are not deductible.

Real estate investors should also be aware of the passive activity loss rules. These rules limit the number of passive losses that investors can deduct against their other income. Passive losses are losses that are generated from activities in which the investor does not materially participate.

For most real estate investors, rental properties are considered passive activities. This means that investors can only deduct passive losses against passive income. If an investor has more passive losses than passive income, they can carry over the excess losses to future years.

However, there are a few exceptions to the passive activity loss rules. For example, real estate investors who meet the material participation test can deduct rental losses against their other income.

The material participation test is met if the investor participates in the rental activity for more than 500 hours per year or more than 100 hours per year if the investor participates in more than one passive activity.

Real estate investors who are unsure whether they qualify for any of the deductions or exceptions listed above should consult with a tax professional.

Here are some additional tips for minimizing income taxes on real estate investments:

- **Keep good records:** It is important to keep good records of all income and expenses related to your real estate investments. This will make it easier to prepare your tax return and take advantage of all of the deductions that you are eligible for.

- **Work with a tax professional:** A tax professional can help you develop a tax strategy that minimizes your taxes and ensures that you comply with all applicable tax laws.

2. Capital gains taxes

Capital gains taxes are one of the most important taxes that real estate investors need to be aware of. Capital gains taxes are paid on the profit that is made when a real estate property is sold. The amount of capital gains tax that is owed depends on how long the investor held the property and the investor's income tax bracket.

Short-term capital gains taxes

If a real estate investor sells a property that they have held for less than one year, the capital gain is considered short-term and is taxed at the investor's regular income tax rate. This means that the investor could owe up to 37% in capital gains taxes.

Long-term capital gains taxes

If a real estate investor sells a property that they have held for at least one year, the capital gain is considered long-term and is taxed at a lower capital gains tax rate. The long-term capital gains tax rates for 2023 are as follows:

- 0% for single filers with taxable income of up to $44,625 and married couples filing jointly with taxable income of up to $89,250

- 15% for single filers with taxable income of $44,626-$492,300 and married couples filing jointly with taxable income of $89,251-$517,200
- 20% for single filers with taxable income over $492,300 and married couples filing jointly with taxable income over $517,200

Net investment income tax (NIIT)

In addition to capital gains taxes, real estate investors with high incomes may also be subject to NIIT. NIIT is a 3.8% tax on net investment income, which includes capital gains. NIIT is only applied to taxpayers with MAGI over a certain threshold. The MAGI thresholds for 2023 are as follows:

- $200,000 for single filers
- $250,000 for married couples filing jointly

How to minimize capital gains taxes on real estate investments

There are several things that real estate investors can do to minimize their capital gains taxes. Some common strategies include:

- **Holding properties for the long term:** The longer an investor holds a property, the lower the capital gains tax rate will be. This is because long-term capital gains are taxed at a lower rate than short-term capital gains.
- **Using a 1031 exchange:** A 1031 exchange allows investors to sell a property and reinvest the proceeds in a similar property without having to pay capital gains taxes. This can be a good way to defer capital gains taxes until a later date.

- **Working with a tax professional:** A tax professional can help real estate investors develop a tax strategy that minimizes their capital gains taxes.

Capital gains taxes can be a significant expense for real estate investors. However, by carefully planning their investments and working with a tax professional, real estate investor can minimize their capital gains taxes and maximize their profits.

3. Property taxes

Property taxes are one of the most significant expenses for real estate investors. Property taxes are assessed by local governments and are based on the value of the property. Property taxes can vary widely from state to state and even from city to city.

How are property taxes calculated?

Property taxes are typically calculated by multiplying the assessed value of the property by the tax rate. The assessed value of the property is determined by the local government and is typically based on the property's purchase price or an appraisal. The tax rate is set by the local government and typically varies depending on the location and type of property.

Who pays property taxes?

The owner of the property is responsible for paying property taxes. However, real estate investors can pass on the cost of property taxes to their tenants by charging them higher rent.

Impact of property taxes on real estate investors

Property taxes can have a significant impact on the profitability of a real estate investment. High property taxes can reduce the amount of cash flow that an investor generates from their rental property. In some cases, property taxes can even make a rental property unprofitable.

How to reduce property taxes

There are several things that real estate investors can do to reduce their property taxes, including:

- **Appeal the assessed value of the property:** If a real estate investor believes that their property has been assessed at too high of a value, they can appeal the assessed value to the local government.
- **Take advantage of property tax exemptions and deductions:** There are several property tax exemptions and deductions that real estate investors may be eligible for. For example, some states offer property tax exemptions for senior citizens and veterans.
- **Make improvements to the property:** Making improvements to a property can increase its value, but it can also increase its assessed value. However, there are some improvements that may qualify for a property tax assessment reduction. For example, some states offer property tax assessment reductions for energy-efficient improvements.

Real estate investors should carefully consider the impact of property taxes when evaluating potential investment properties. By understanding how property taxes are calculated and knowing how to reduce property taxes, real estate investors can maximize their profits

Other real estate investment taxes

In addition to the taxes listed above, real estate investors may also be subject to other taxes, such as:

1. Self-employment tax: Self-employment tax is a social security tax that is paid by self-employed individuals, including real estate investors who manage their own rental properties. Self-employment tax is paid on net self-employment earnings, which is the total net income from a self-employed business minus certain deductions, such as the cost of goods sold and business expenses.

The self-employment tax rate is 15.3% for 2023, which includes 12.4% for Social Security and 2.9% for Medicare. The Social Security portion of the self-employment tax is only applied to the first $147,000 of net self-employment earnings in 2023. The Medicare portion of self-employment tax is applied to all net self-employment earnings.

Real estate investors who are subject to self-employment tax must pay estimated taxes throughout the year. Estimated taxes are quarterly payments of income tax and self-employment tax that are based on your estimated income and tax liability for the year.

If you are a real estate investor who manages your own rental properties, you may be able to deduct certain business expenses from your net self-employment earnings. Some common deductible expenses include:

- Advertising
- Commissions and fees
- Home office expenses
- Insurance
- Legal and professional fees
- Mortgage interest

- Office supplies
- Repairs and maintenance
- Travel expenses

By deducting allowable business expenses, you can reduce your net self-employment earnings and your self-employment tax liability.

If you are a real estate investor who is subject to self-employment tax, it is important to file a Schedule C with your annual income tax return. Schedule C is used to report income and expenses from a self-employed business.

You can also use Schedule SE to calculate your self-employment tax liability. Schedule SE is used to calculate the Social Security and Medicare taxes that are owed on self-employment earnings.

If you have any questions about self-employment tax, you should consult with a tax professional. A tax professional can help you to determine if you are subject to self-employment tax and help you to file the necessary tax forms.

Here are some additional tips for dealing with self-employment tax as a real estate investor:

- Keep good records of all your business income and expenses. This will help you to accurately calculate your net self-employment earnings and your self-employment tax liability.
- Pay estimated taxes throughout the year. This will help you to avoid a large tax bill at the end of the year.
- File a Schedule C and Schedule SE with your annual income tax return. This will help you to ensure that you are in compliance with all applicable tax laws.

- Work with a tax professional to minimize your self-employment tax liability.

2. Net investment income tax (NIIT): The Net Investment Income Tax (NIIT) is a 3.8% tax on net investment income of individuals, estates, and trusts with modified adjusted gross income (MAGI) above certain threshold amounts. Net investment income includes interest, dividends, capital gains, rental income, and non-qualified annuities.

The NIIT was introduced by the Affordable Care Act in 2013 to help fund healthcare initiatives. It is important to note that the NIIT is an additional tax on net investment income, and it is paid in addition to regular income taxes.

Calculating NIIT

The NIIT is calculated on the lesser of the following two amounts:

- Net investment income
- The amount by which MAGI exceeds the applicable threshold amount

The MAGI threshold amounts for 2023 are as follows:

- Single filer: $200,000
- Married filing jointly: $250,000
- Head of household: $225,000
- Estates and trusts: $13,450

Example

Suppose a single taxpayer has MAGI of $210,000 and net investment income of $25,000. The taxpayer's NIIT would be calculated as follows:

Lesser of:

Net investment income: $25,000

MAGI minus threshold amount: $210,000 - $200,000 = $10,000

NIIT: $10,000 * 3.8% = $380

Avoiding NIIT

There are a few ways to avoid the NIIT:

1. **Reduce net investment income:** This can be done by selling investments that are generating high levels of income, such as dividend-paying stocks or bonds. Investors can also invest in tax-advantaged accounts, such as retirement accounts or health savings accounts.
2. **Reduce MAGI:** This can be done by taking advantage of deductions, such as charitable contributions or mortgage interest. Investors can also contribute to tax-advantaged accounts, such as retirement accounts or health savings accounts.
3. **Invest in qualified investments:** Certain types of investments are exempt from NIIT, such as municipal bonds and qualified business income (QBI).

The NIIT is an important tax to be aware of for real estate investors. Real estate investors can avoid NIIT by reducing their net investment income, reducing their MAGI, or investing in qualified investments.

3. Real estate transfer tax: Real estate transfer tax (RETT) is a tax that is imposed on the transfer of real property from one owner to another. RETT is typically assessed by local governments, such as counties or municipalities. The amount of RETT varies from jurisdiction to jurisdiction, but it is typically a percentage of the purchase price of the property.

In the United States, RETT is one of the most common types of real estate taxes. It is estimated that RETT generates over $20 billion in revenue for local governments each year.

Who pays RETT?

RETT is typically paid by the buyer of the property. However, the buyer and seller may agree to split the cost of RETT, or the seller may agree to pay the entire cost.

How is RETT calculated?

The amount of RETT is calculated by multiplying the purchase price of the property by the RETT rate. The RETT rate varies from jurisdiction to jurisdiction, but it is typically between 1% and 3% of the purchase price.

Examples of RETT rates in different jurisdictions:

- New York City: 0.45% to 1.45%, depending on the purchase price
- Los Angeles County: 0.55%
- Miami-Dade County: 0.65%
- Chicago: 0.75%
- Houston: 0.25%

How to pay RETT

RETT is typically paid at closing. The buyer and seller will typically sign a document called a deed transfer tax affidavit, which states how much RETT is owed and who is responsible for paying it. The escrow company will then pay the RETT to the local government on behalf of the buyer and seller.

Exemptions from RETT

There are a few exemptions from RETT, such as transfers of property between spouses, parents, and children, and charitable organizations. However, the specific exemptions vary from jurisdiction to jurisdiction.

Impact of RETT on real estate investors

RETT can be a significant cost for real estate investors. However, there are a few things that investors can do to minimize the impact of RETT, such as:

1. **Negotiating the purchase price:** Investors should negotiate the purchase price of the property with the seller. If the seller is willing to lower the purchase price, the investor will pay less RETT.
2. **Structuring the transaction:** Investors may be able to structure the transaction in a way that reduces or eliminates RETT. For example, investors may be able to purchase the property through a pass-through entity, such as an LLC or S corporation.
3. **Claiming deductions:** Investors may be able to claim deductions for RETT on their tax returns. However, it is important to consult with a tax advisor to determine if you are eligible for these deductions.

Overall, RETT is an important tax that real estate investors should be aware of. By understanding how RETT is calculated and paid, and by taking steps to minimize its impact, investors can save money on their real estate investments.

8.2. How to minimize your real estate investment taxes

There are a number of ways to minimize your real estate investment taxes. Here are some tips:

1. Take advantage of all deductible expenses. Real estate investors can deduct a wide range of expenses, including mortgage interest, property taxes, insurance, repairs and maintenance, depreciation, and travel expenses related to your rental properties. Be sure to keep good records of all your expenses so you can deduct them on your tax return.

2. Structure your business as a pass-through entity. Pass-through entities, such as sole proprietorships, partnerships, LLCs, and S corporations, allow business income to pass through to the owners' individual tax returns. This can help to avoid double taxation, which is when income is taxed at the business level and then again at the individual level.

3. Use a depreciation schedule to deduct the cost of your rental properties over time. Depreciation is a non-cash expense, which means it reduces your taxable income without actually costing you any money.

4. Defer capital gains taxes by selling your rental properties in installments. If you sell a rental property for a profit, you can defer capital gains taxes by selling it in installments over a period of years. This can be a good option if you are planning to reinvest the proceeds from the sale into another rental property.

5. Consider forming a real estate investment trust (REIT). REITs are companies that own and operate income-producing real estate. REITs are not taxed at the corporate level, so shareholders receive 90% or more of the company's taxable income in the form of dividends.

Here are some additional tips for minimizing your real estate investment taxes:

1. Work with an accountant who specializes in real estate taxes. A qualified accountant can help you to identify all the tax deductions and credits that you are eligible for, and can also help you to avoid any costly tax mistakes.

2. Keep good records of all your income and expenses. This will make it much easier to file your tax return and claim all of your deductions.

3. Plan ahead for your tax liability. By estimating your tax liability early in the year, you can take steps to reduce it, such as making estimated tax payments or selling underperforming properties.

By following these tips, you can minimize your real estate investment taxes and maximize your profits.

8.3. How to work with a tax accountant to file your real estate investment taxes

Working with a tax accountant to file your real estate investment taxes can help you ensure that you are in compliance with all applicable tax laws and that you are taking advantage of all available deductions. Here are some tips for working with a tax accountant to file your real estate investment taxes:

1. Choose a tax accountant who has experience with real estate investors. Real estate investment taxes can be complex, so it is important to choose a tax accountant who has experience with real estate investors. Ask the tax accountant about their experience with real estate investors and whether they are familiar with the specific tax laws that apply to real estate investments.

2. Gather all of your tax documents. Before you meet with your tax accountant, gather all of your tax documents, including your rental income statements, property tax bills, and mortgage interest statements. You should also gather any other relevant documents, such as depreciation schedules and receipts for deductible expenses.

3. Organize your tax documents. Once you have gathered all of your tax documents, organize them so that your tax accountant can easily find them. This will help to save time and money during your tax preparation appointment.

4. Be prepared to answer questions. Your tax accountant will likely have a number of questions about your real estate investments and your income and expenses. Be prepared to answer these questions accurately and completely.

5. Review your tax return carefully. Before you sign your tax return, be sure to review it carefully to ensure that it is accurate and complete. Ask your tax accountant to explain any items that you do not understand.

Here are some additional tips for working with a tax accountant to file your real estate investment taxes:

1. Communicate with your tax accountant regularly. Don't wait until the last minute to contact your tax accountant. If you have any questions about your real estate investments or your taxes, contact your tax accountant as soon as possible.

2. Keep your tax accountant informed of any changes. If you make any changes to your real estate investments, such as buying or selling a property, be sure to inform your tax accountant as soon as possible. This will help your tax accountant to prepare your tax return accurately.

3. Take advantage of your tax accountant's expertise. Your tax accountant can provide you with valuable advice on how to minimize your real estate investment taxes and how to structure your investments in a tax-efficient manner.

Working with a tax accountant to file your real estate investment taxes can help you save time and money and ensure that you are in compliance with all applicable tax laws. By following the tips above, you can make the most of your relationship with your tax accountant and maximize your profits.

Chapter 9: Real Estate Investing Mistakes to Avoid

9.1. The most common real estate investing mistakes

Real estate investing can be a great way to generate income and build wealth, but it is important to be aware of the common mistakes that new investors make. Here are some of the most common real estate investing mistakes:

1, Not doing enough research: Before investing in any property, it is important to do your research and understand the local real estate market. This includes factors such as property values, rental rates, and vacancy rates.

2. Overpaying for a property: It is important to pay a fair price for any investment property. Overpaying for a property can make it difficult to generate a profit.

3. Not factoring in all of the costs: When calculating the potential return on investment for a property, it is important to factor in all of the costs associated with owning and operating the property. This includes things like mortgage payments, property taxes, insurance, and maintenance costs.

4. Neglecting maintenance and repairs: It is important to maintain your investment properties in good condition. This will help to protect your investment and attract and retain tenants.

5. Not screening tenants carefully: It is important to carefully screen tenants before renting to them. This will help to reduce the risk of evictions and other problems.

6. Not having a plan for managing the property: If you are not planning to manage the property yourself, it is important to have a plan in place for how the property will be managed. This may involve hiring a property manager or joining a real estate investment trust (REIT).

Here are some additional tips to avoid making common real estate investing mistakes:

1. Get pre-approved for a mortgage: This will give you an idea of how much money you can borrow and what your monthly mortgage payments will be.

2. Work with a qualified real estate agent: A good real estate agent can help you to find the right property for your investment goals and budget.

3. Have the property inspected by a qualified home inspector: This will help to identify any potential problems with the property before you buy it.

4. Create a business plan for your investment property: This will help you to track your income and expenses and ensure that you are meeting your financial goals.

9.2. How to avoid making these mistakes

To avoid the common real estate investing mistakes discussed above, you can follow these tips:

1. Do your research.

This includes understanding the local real estate market, the different types of investment properties, and the risks and rewards of real estate investing. You should also research specific properties before you buy them. This includes reviewing the property's history, condition, and financial potential.

2. Don't overpay.

One of the best ways to avoid overpaying for a property is to get a pre-approval for a mortgage before you start shopping. This will give you an idea of how much money you can borrow and what your monthly mortgage payments will be. It's also important to do your research on comparable properties in the area to get a sense of what the property is worth.

3. Factor in all the costs.

In addition to the purchase price of the property, you'll also need to factor in the costs of closing costs, mortgage payments, property taxes, insurance, maintenance, and repairs. It's important to have a realistic budget for your investment property so that you can make sure that it's profitable.

4. Don't neglect maintenance and repairs.

A well-maintained property is more likely to attract and retain tenants, and it's also less likely to have major problems down the road. Be sure to budget for regular maintenance and repairs, and be prepared to address any unexpected problems that arise.

5. Screen tenants carefully.

Before you rent to a tenant, be sure to screen them carefully. This includes checking their credit history, rental history, and employment history. You should also interview the tenant to get a sense of their character and responsibility.

6. Have a plan for managing the property.

If you're not planning to manage the property yourself, you'll need to have a plan in place for how it will be managed. This may involve hiring a property manager or joining a real estate investment trust (REIT).

Here are some additional tips to avoid making common real estate investing mistakes:

1. Don't rush into a deal. Take your time to find the right property and negotiate the best possible deal.
2. Don't be afraid to walk away from a deal. If you're not comfortable with a property or the terms of the deal, don't be afraid to walk away. There are other investment opportunities out there.
3. Work with a team of professionals. This includes a real estate agent, a mortgage broker, an attorney, and a property manager. A good team of professionals can help you to avoid making mistakes and make the most of your investment.

By following these tips, you can increase your chances of success as a real estate investor.

9.3. What to do if you make a real estate investing mistake

Real estate investing is a complex and challenging endeavor, and even the most experienced investors make mistakes. If you find yourself in the situation of having made a real estate investing mistake, here are some steps you can take to minimize your losses and move forward:

1. Acknowledge the mistake. The first step is to acknowledge that you have made a mistake. This may be difficult, but it is important to be honest with yourself and to face the problem head-on.

2. Assess the damage. Once you have acknowledged the mistake, take some time to assess the damage. This includes understanding the financial implications of the mistake, as well as the impact on your investment goals.

3. Develop a plan. Once you have assessed the damage, develop a plan to address the mistake and minimize your losses. This may involve selling the property, refinancing the mortgage, or renting out the property.

4. Learn from your mistakes. Every mistake is an opportunity to learn. Take some time to reflect on what you did wrong and how you can avoid making the same mistake in the future.

Here are some additional tips for dealing with real estate investing mistakes:

1. Don't panic. It is important to stay calm and collected when you make a mistake. Panicking will only make the situation worse.

2. Don't be afraid to ask for help. There are many people who can help you deal with a real estate investing mistake, such as real estate agents, attorneys, and financial advisors.

3. Don't give up. Even if you make a big mistake, it is important to not give up on real estate investing. Everyone makes mistakes, and the most successful investors are the ones who learn from their mistakes and move on.

Here are some specific examples of what you can do if you make a common real estate investing mistake:

1. If you overpaid for a property: You may be able to negotiate a lower price with the seller, or you may need to wait until the market improves before you can sell the property for a profit.

2. If you neglected maintenance and repairs: This can be costly to fix, but it is important to address any maintenance issues as soon as possible. You may also be able to claim some of the repair costs as tax deductions.

3. If you didn't screen tenants carefully: If you have a tenant who is not paying rent or is damaging the property, you may need to evict them. This can be a time-consuming and expensive process, but it is important to protect your investment.

4. If you didn't have a plan for managing the property: If you are unable to manage the property yourself, you may need to hire a property manager. This can be a good option if you don't have the time or expertise to manage the property yourself.

Making a real estate investing mistake can be discouraging, but it is important to remember that everyone makes mistakes. The important thing is to learn from your mistakes and move on. By following the tips above, you can minimize your losses and get back on track to achieving your investment goals.

Chapter 10: Building a Real Estate Investment Team

10.1. The different members of a real estate investment team

A real estate investment team is a group of professionals who work together to help real estate investors achieve their goals. The specific members of a real estate investment team can vary depending on the investor's needs and the type of investments they are making. However, some common members of a real estate investment team include:

1. Real estate agent: Real estate agents are one of the most common members of a real estate investment team. They can play a vital role in helping investors to find and purchase properties, negotiate the purchase price, and navigate the closing process.

Here are some of the specific ways that a real estate agent can help real estate investors:

- **Find investment properties:** Real estate agents have access to a wide network of properties, including many that are not publicly listed. This gives investors access to a wider range of potential investment properties than they would be able to find on their own.
- **Evaluate investment properties:** Real estate agents can help investors evaluate potential investment properties by providing them with information on the local real estate market, property values, and rental rates. This information can help investors to make informed decisions about which properties to purchase.

- **Negotiate the purchase price:** Real estate agents are skilled negotiators who can help investors to get the best possible price on the properties they purchase.
- **Navigate the closing process:** The closing process can be complex and time-consuming. Real estate agents can help investors to navigate the closing process smoothly and efficiently.

In addition to these specific tasks, real estate agents can also provide investors with general guidance and support on their real estate investment journey. They can help investors to understand the real estate market, to develop investment strategies, and to avoid common mistakes.

2. Real estate attorney: A real estate attorney is one of the most important members of a real estate investment team. They can help investors to understand and protect their legal interests in real estate transactions.

Here are some of the specific ways that a real estate attorney can help real estate investors:

- **Review and negotiate real estate contracts:** Real estate attorneys can review and negotiate real estate contracts on behalf of investors. This helps to ensure that investors understand their rights and obligations under the contract and that the contract is in their best interests.
- **Conduct title searches:** Real estate attorneys can conduct title searches to identify any potential liens or encumbrances on a property. This helps to protect investors from buying a property with hidden problems.

- **Draft and review closing documents:** Real estate attorneys can draft and review closing documents for investors. This includes documents such as the deed, mortgage, and title insurance policy.
- **Handle closings:** Real estate attorneys can handle closings on behalf of investors. This includes disbursing funds, transferring title, and recording the deed.
- **Represent investors in legal disputes:** If an investor becomes involved in a legal dispute related to a real estate transaction, their attorney can represent them in court.

In addition to providing these specific services, real estate attorneys can also provide general legal advice to real estate investors. This can include advice on tax implications, zoning laws, and landlord-tenant law.

Hiring a real estate attorney is essential for any real estate investor. A good real estate attorney can help investors to avoid legal pitfalls and to protect their assets.

3. Real estate accountant: A real estate accountant is a professional who specializes in accounting and taxation for real estate investors. Real estate accountants can help investors with a variety of tasks, including:

- Tracking income and expenses
- Preparing tax returns
- Developing financial strategies
- Managing cash flow
- Analyzing investment opportunities
- Advising on tax implications of real estate transactions

Real estate accountants play an important role on real estate investment teams. They can help investors to save money on taxes, make sound financial decisions, and avoid costly mistakes.

Here are some of the specific ways that a real estate accountant can help real estate investors:

- **Minimize taxes:** Real estate accountants can help investors identify and claim all of the tax deductions and credits that they are eligible for. They can also help investors to structure their investments in a way that minimizes their tax liability.
- **Make sound financial decisions:** Real estate accountants can help investors develop financial projections and to analyze investment opportunities. They can also help investors assess the risks and rewards of different investment strategies.
- **Avoid costly mistakes:** Real estate accountants can help investors to avoid making common tax and financial mistakes. They can also help investors to stay in compliance with all applicable tax laws.

Real estate accountants are a valuable resource for real estate investors. By working with a qualified real estate accountant, investors can save money on taxes, make sound financial decisions, and avoid costly mistakes.

4. Property manager: A property manager is a professional who is responsible for the day-to-day management of rental properties. Property managers typically handle a wide range of tasks, including:

- Finding tenants
- Screening tenants
- Collecting rent
- Handling maintenance and repairs

- Enforcement of lease agreements
- Evictions (if necessary)
- Financial reporting

Property managers can be a valuable asset to real estate investors, as they can free up investors' time and allow them to focus on other aspects of their business. Property managers can also help investors to maximize their rental income and minimize their expenses.

Here are some of the key benefits of hiring a property manager:

- **They save you time and hassle:** Property managers can handle all of the day-to-day tasks associated with managing rental properties, so you don't have to. This can free up your time so that you can focus on other aspects of your business or personal life.
- **They help you to attract and retain quality tenants:** Property managers have the experience and expertise to find and screen quality tenants. They also know how to draft and enforce lease agreements that protect your interests as a landlord.
- **They help you to maximize your rental income:** Property managers know how to set competitive rental rates and collect rent on time and in full. They can also help you to identify and implement ways to increase your rental income, such as by making minor improvements to your properties.
- **They help you to minimize your expenses:** Property managers have relationships with qualified contractors and vendors, which can help you save money on maintenance and repairs. They can also help you to

identify and implement ways to reduce your operating expenses, such as by negotiating lower insurance rates.

- **They help you to stay compliant with the law:** Property managers are familiar with the latest laws and regulations that apply to landlords. This can help you to avoid costly legal problems down the road.

If you are a real estate investor, hiring a property manager can be a wise decision. Property managers can help you to save time and money, maximize your rental income, and minimize your risks.

5. Contractor: Contractors are one of the most important members of a real estate investment team. They are responsible for making repairs and renovations to investment properties. This can include tasks such as:

- Fixing broken plumbing or electrical systems
- Repairing or replacing damaged roofing or siding
- Updating kitchens and bathrooms
- Painting and flooring
- Adding or removing walls
- Converting properties into multi-unit dwellings

Contractors can also help investors to prepare properties for sale. This may involve making minor repairs and cosmetic updates, as well as staging the property to make it more appealing to potential buyers.

When choosing a contractor for your real estate investment team, it is important to consider the following factors:

- **Experience:** Choose a contractor with experience in the type of work that you need done. For example, if you are renovating a rental property, you will want to choose a contractor with experience in residential construction.

- **License and insurance:** Make sure that the contractor is licensed and insured. This will help to protect you in case of any problems with the work.
- **References:** Ask the contractor for references from previous clients. This will give you an idea of the quality of their work and their customer service.
- **Price:** Get estimates from multiple contractors before choosing one. Be sure to compare the prices and services offered by each contractor.

Once you have chosen a contractor, it is important to communicate your expectations clearly. Be sure to provide them with a detailed scope of work and a budget. It is also important to inspect the work regularly to ensure that it is being done to your satisfaction.

Here are some tips for working with contractors on your real estate investment team:

- **Be clear about your expectations:** Before you start working with a contractor, be sure to clearly communicate your expectations. This includes the scope of work, the budget, and the timeline.
- **Get everything in writing:** Once you have agreed on the scope of work and the budget, be sure to get everything in writing. This will help to avoid any misunderstandings down the road.
- **Inspect the work regularly:** It is important to inspect the work regularly to ensure that it is being done to your satisfaction. Be sure to point out any problems immediately so that they can be corrected.

- **Pay the contractor on time:** It is important to pay the contractor on time according to the agreed-upon payment schedule. This will help to maintain a good relationship with the contractor and ensure that they complete the work on time and on budget.

Working with a qualified contractor is essential for success as a real estate investor. By following the tips above, you can build a strong relationship with your contractor and ensure that your investment properties are well-maintained and repaired.

6. Financial advisor: A financial advisor is a professional who can help you with your financial planning, including your real estate investments. They can help you to:

- **Define your financial goals:** What do you want to achieve with your real estate investments? Do you want to generate income, build wealth, or both? A financial advisor can help you define your goals and develop a plan to achieve them.
- **Assess your risk tolerance:** How much risk are you comfortable with? Real estate investing can be a risky investment, so it is important to understand your risk tolerance and to invest accordingly. A financial advisor can help you assess your risk tolerance and develop an investment strategy that is right for you.
- **Allocate your assets:** How much of your portfolio should you allocate to real estate? A financial advisor can help you to develop an asset allocation plan that meets your investment goals and risk tolerance.
- **Choose the right real estate investments:** There are many different types of real estate investments available. A financial advisor can help you to choose the right investments for your goals and risk tolerance.

- **Manage your real estate investments:** Once you have purchased real estate investments, you need to manage them effectively. This includes tracking your income and expenses, making necessary repairs and renovations, and finding and screening tenants. A financial advisor can help you to manage your real estate investments and to ensure that you are meeting your financial goals.

In addition to the above, a financial advisor can also help you with the following:

- **Tax planning:** Real estate investing can have complex tax implications. A financial advisor can help you to develop a tax plan that minimizes your tax liability.
- **Estate planning:** Your real estate investments should be included in your overall estate plan. A financial advisor can help you develop an estate plan that ensures that your assets are distributed according to your wishes after you die.

Hiring a financial advisor can be a valuable investment for real estate investors. A financial advisor can help you to make sound financial decisions and to achieve your investment goals.

In addition to these core members, a real estate investment team may also include other professionals, such as:

1. Hard money lender: A hard money lender is a private lender who provides short-term loans to real estate investors. Hard money loans are typically used to finance the purchase and renovation of investment properties. Hard money lenders tend to be more flexible than traditional banks and can often close loans quickly, which can be important for real estate investors who need to act quickly on a deal.

How hard money loans work

Hard money lenders typically base their loans on the value of the property, rather than the borrower's credit score. This makes hard money loans a good option for real estate investors who have poor credit or who are new to real estate investing.

Hard money loans are typically for a shorter term than traditional bank loans, ranging from one to three years. Hard money lenders also typically charge higher interest rates than traditional banks. However, the higher interest rates can be justified by the convenience and flexibility of hard money loans.

When to use a hard money lender

Hard money loans can be a good option for real estate investors in a number of situations, such as:

- When purchasing a property that needs to be renovated before it can be rented or sold.
- When purchasing a property at auction.
- When financing a fix-and-flip deal.
- When financing a rental property.

Advantages of using a hard money lender

There are a number of advantages to using a hard money lender, including:

- **Flexibility:** Hard money lenders are typically more flexible than traditional banks and can often close loans quickly.

- **Speed:** Hard money lenders can often close loans in a matter of days or weeks, while traditional banks can take weeks or even months to close a loan.
- **No credit score requirement:** Hard money lenders typically do not require borrowers to have a good credit score.
- **Ability to finance properties that need renovation:** Hard money lenders are often willing to finance properties that need renovation, which can be difficult to do with a traditional bank loan.

Disadvantages of using a hard money lender

There are also a few disadvantages to using a hard money lender, including:

- **Higher interest rates:** Hard money lenders typically charge higher interest rates than traditional banks.
- **Shorter loan terms:** Hard money loans are typically for a shorter term than traditional bank loans.
- **Fees:** Hard money lenders may charge additional fees, such as origination fees and prepayment penalties.

How to find a hard money lender

There are a number of ways to find a hard money lender, including:

- Asking for referrals from other real estate investors.
- Searching online directories of hard money lenders.
- Attending real estate investment events.
- Networking with other real estate professionals.

When considering using a hard money lender, it is important to do your research and compare different lenders before choosing one. Be sure to ask about the lender's interest rates, fees, and loan terms. It is also important to make sure that the lender is licensed and insured.

2. Real estate syndicator: A real estate syndicator is a person or company that raises capital from investors to purchase and manage real estate properties. Syndicators typically have a deep understanding of the real estate market and a proven track record of success. They are responsible for identifying and evaluating potential investment properties, underwriting the deals, and structuring the syndications.

Syndicators also play a key role in managing the investment properties on behalf of their investors. This includes tasks such as finding and screening tenants, collecting rent, handling maintenance and repairs, and overseeing renovations. Syndicators typically charge a fee for their services, which is typically a percentage of the raised capital and a share of the profits.

Real estate syndicators can be valuable members of a real estate investment team for a number of reasons. First, they provide investors with access to investment opportunities that they may not be able to access on their own. For example, syndicators may be able to purchase large commercial properties or multi-family apartment buildings that are out of the reach of individual investors.

Second, syndicators provide investors with a way to invest in real estate without having to manage the properties themselves. This can be a major benefit for investors who do not have the time or expertise to manage real estate properties.

Third, syndicators can help investors to diversify their real estate portfolios. For example, a syndicator may offer a variety of syndications that invest in different types of properties, such as office buildings, apartment buildings, and retail centers. This allows investors to spread their risk across different property types and markets.

When choosing a real estate syndicator, it is important to consider their experience, track record, and investment philosophy. It is also important to understand the terms and fees of the syndication before investing.

3. Real estate coach or mentor: A real estate coach or mentor is a valuable member of a real estate investment team. They can provide investors with guidance, support, and accountability on their real estate investment journey.

Here are some of the benefits of working with a real estate coach or mentor:

- They can help you to set and achieve your real estate investment goals. A real estate coach or mentor can help you develop a realistic investment plan and identify the strategies and resources that you need to achieve your goals.
- They can help you to learn about the real estate market and how to invest profitably. A real estate coach or mentor can teach you about the different types of real estate investments, how to find good deals, and how to manage your investments.
- They can help you to avoid common real estate investing mistakes. A real estate coach or mentor can share their knowledge and experience with you so that you can avoid the mistakes that they made.
- They can provide you with motivation and support. Real estate investing can be challenging, but a real estate

coach or mentor can be there to support you and help you stay motivated.

When choosing a real estate coach or mentor, it is important to find someone who has a proven track record of success in real estate investing. You should also choose someone who is a good fit for your personality and investment goals.

Working with a real estate coach or mentor can be a great investment in your success as a real estate investor. By providing you with guidance, support, and accountability, a real estate coach or mentor can help you to achieve your investment goals more quickly and easily.

Here are some specific ways that a real estate coach or mentor can help you:

- Help you to develop a business plan for your real estate investments. This includes identifying your investment goals, target market, and strategies for finding and acquiring properties.
- Teach you how to analyze real estate deals. This includes understanding the key financial metrics, such as cash flow and return on investment (ROI).
- Help you to negotiate and close on real estate deals. This includes understanding the legal and financial aspects of real estate transactions.
- Provide you with support and guidance as you manage your real estate investments. This includes helping you to find and screen tenants, handling maintenance and repairs, and tracking your income and expenses.

If you are serious about success as a real estate investor, consider working with a real estate coach or mentor. They can be a valuable asset to your team and help you to achieve your investment goals more quickly and easily.

Building a strong real estate investment team is essential for success. By working with a team of qualified professionals, investors can minimize their risks and maximize their chances of success.

Here are some tips for building a real estate investment team:

1. Start by building a network of real estate professionals. This can be done by attending industry events, joining online forums, and reaching out to people you know who are involved in real estate.

2. Once you have a network of real estate professionals, start to interview potential candidates for your team. Be sure to ask about their experience, qualifications, and fees.

3. Choose team members who are a good fit for your personality and investment goals. It is important to have a team that you can trust and rely on.

4. Communicate regularly with your team members and keep them updated on your investment goals and progress.

5. Be prepared to compensate your team members fairly for their services.

10.2. How to find and work with a real estate agent

To find and work with a real estate agent, you can follow these steps:

1. Ask for referrals: Asking for referrals is one of the best ways to find a qualified and trustworthy real estate agent. When you ask people, you know and respect for referrals, you are getting their personal recommendations for agents who have helped them in the past. This can save you a lot of time and effort in your search for a real estate agent.

To ask for referrals, you can start by talking to your friends, family, and colleagues. You can also ask your mortgage broker or lender for recommendations. If you know any other real estate investors, you can ask them for referrals as well.

Once you have a few names of potential real estate agents, you can start interviewing them. Be sure to ask about the agent's experience, qualifications, and fees. You should also ask about the agent's specialty, as some agents specialize in working with buyers, while others specialize in working with sellers.

Here are some tips for asking for referrals:

- Be specific about your needs and goals. When you ask for referrals, let people know what you are looking for in a real estate agent. For example, you can mention the type of property you are interested in buying or selling, the area you are interested in, and your budget.
- Be clear about what you are looking for in an agent. Let people know what is important to you in a real estate agent, such as experience, communication skills, and negotiation skills.
- Be grateful. When someone gives you a referral, be sure to thank them. You can send a thank-you note or email, or you can simply call them to express your gratitude.

By following these tips, you can increase your chances of getting referrals from people you know and trust. This can help you to find a qualified and trustworthy real estate agent who can help you achieve your real estate goals.

Here are some additional benefits of asking for referrals:

- Referrals are more likely to be qualified. When you ask people for referrals, you are getting recommendations for agents who have already been vetted by someone you know and trust. This means that you are more likely to find a qualified and competent agent.
- Referrals are more likely to be a good fit for you. When you ask people for referrals, you are getting recommendations for agents who have a similar personality and style to the people you know and trust. This means that you are more likely to find an agent that you feel comfortable with and that you can build a good working relationship with.
- Referrals can save you time and effort. Asking for referrals can save you a lot of time and effort in your search for a real estate agent. Instead of having to research different agents and interview them yourself, you can get recommendations from people you know and trust.

Overall, asking for referrals is a great way to find a qualified and trustworthy real estate agent who can help you achieve your real estate goals.

2. Interview potential agents: Interviewing potential real estate agents is one of the most important steps in finding the right agent to help you with your real estate transaction. When interviewing agents, be sure to ask about their experience, qualifications, fees, and specialty. You should also ask about their approach to real estate and their communication style.

Here are some specific questions you can ask potential real estate agents during your interviews:

- How many years of experience do you have as a real estate agent?
- What is your area of specialization?
- What is your track record of success?
- What is your commission rate?
- What is your communication style?
- How do you stay up-to-date on the real estate market?
- How would you describe your approach to real estate?
- What are your thoughts on the current real estate market?
- What are your strengths and weaknesses as a real estate agent?
- Can you provide me with references from previous clients?

In addition to asking questions, it is also important to pay attention to the agent's demeanor and professionalism. Do they seem knowledgeable and experienced? Are they easy to talk to? Do they answer your questions clearly and concisely? Do they seem genuinely interested in helping you achieve your real estate goals?

By interviewing potential real estate agents, you can get a better sense of who they are and how they work. This will help you to choose the right agent to represent you in your real estate transaction.

Here are some additional tips for interviewing potential real estate agents:

- Prepare a list of questions ahead of time. This will help you to make the most of your interview time and to gather all of the information you need to make a decision.

- Schedule interviews with multiple agents. This will give you a chance to compare and contrast different agents and to find the one that is the best fit for you.
- Be honest and upfront about your needs and goals. This will help the agents to better understand what you are looking for and to provide you with the best possible service.
- Trust your gut instinct. If you feel comfortable with an agent and you trust them to represent your interests, then that is a good sign.

3. Choose an agent you feel comfortable with: Choosing a real estate agent you feel comfortable with is one of the most important steps in finding and working with a real estate agent. You will be working closely with this agent throughout your real estate transaction, so it is important to choose someone you like and respect.

Here are some factors to consider when choosing a real estate agent that you feel comfortable with:

- **Communication style:** Do you feel comfortable communicating with the agent? Are they responsive to your calls and emails? Do they take the time to listen to your needs and concerns?
- **Personality:** Do you have a good rapport with the agent? Do you feel like you can be yourself around them?
- **Expertise:** Does the agent have the necessary expertise and experience to help you with your real estate transaction?

- **Reputation:** What is the agent's reputation in the community? Have they helped other clients achieve their real estate goals?

It is also important to trust your gut instinct. If you have a good feeling about an agent, that is a good sign.

Here are some tips for building rapport with a real estate agent:

- Be open and honest about your needs and goals.
- Be responsive to the agent's calls and emails.
- Ask questions and seek clarification.
- Be respectful of the agent's time and expertise.
- Be willing to compromise.

By following these tips, you can choose a real estate agent that you feel comfortable with and that you trust. This will help you to have a positive and successful real estate experience.

Here are some additional benefits of choosing a real estate agent that you feel comfortable with:

- **Smoother transaction:** When you feel comfortable with your real estate agent, the entire transaction will be smoother and less stressful. You will be more likely to ask questions, share your concerns, and be open to the agent's suggestions.
- **Better communication:** When you feel comfortable with your real estate agent, communication will be more effective. You will be more likely to share important information and to understand the agent's feedback.

- **Stronger relationship:** When you feel comfortable with your real estate agent, you will develop a stronger relationship with them. This can be beneficial in the long run, as you may need to work with the agent again in the future or you may want to refer them to your friends and family.

Once you have chosen a real estate agent, you can start working together to find the right property for you or to sell your property. Your agent will help you to navigate the real estate market and to negotiate the best possible price for your property.

Here are some tips for working with a real estate agent:

1. Be clear about your needs and goals. Make sure to communicate your needs and goals to your agent as clearly as possible. This will help the agent to find the right properties for you or to market your property effectively.
2. Be responsive. When your agent contacts you, be sure to respond promptly. This will help to keep the process moving forward.
3. Be honest and transparent. Be honest and transparent with your agent about your finances and your expectations. This will help the agent to better serve you.
4. Be prepared to compromise. It is unlikely that you will find the perfect property or that you will get the perfect price for your property. Be prepared to compromise on some things.
5. Trust your agent. You have chosen your real estate agent because you trust them. Trust them to do their best to represent your interests.

By following these tips, you can build a successful relationship with your real estate agent and achieve your real estate goals.

10.3. How to find and work with a real estate attorney

To find and work with a real estate attorney, you can follow these steps:

1. Ask for referrals: Asking for referrals is one of the best ways to find a qualified real estate attorney. When you ask for referrals, you are getting recommendations from people you trust, such as friends, family, colleagues, and other real estate investors. These people have likely had personal experience with real estate attorneys, so they can provide you with valuable insights and recommendations.

Here are some tips for asking for referrals for a real estate attorney:

- Be specific about what you are looking for. When you ask for referrals, be sure to specify what type of real estate attorney you are looking for. For example, if you are buying a home, you will want to find an attorney who specializes in residential real estate transactions. If you are selling a business, you will want to find an attorney who specializes in business law.
- Ask people you trust. Only ask for referrals from people you trust and respect. This could include friends, family, colleagues, or other real estate investors. You may also want to ask your mortgage broker or lender for recommendations.
- Get multiple referrals. Don't just rely on one referral. Try to get referrals from several different people. This

will give you a better selection of attorneys to choose from.

Once you have a few referrals, you can start interviewing potential attorneys. Be sure to ask about the attorney's experience, qualifications, and fees. You should also ask about the attorney's specialty and whether they have any experience with the type of real estate transaction you are involved in.

Here are some questions you can ask when interviewing potential real estate attorneys:

- How many years of experience do you have in real estate law?
- What types of real estate transactions do you specialize in?
- Have you handled any real estate transactions similar to mine?
- What are your fees?
- What is your communication style?
- What is your availability?

2. Interview potential attorneys: Once you have a few referrals, interview each attorney to see who is the best fit for you. Here are some questions you can ask:

- What is your experience with real estate law? Find out how long the attorney has been practicing real estate law and how many real estate transactions they have handled. You may also want to ask about their experience with the specific type of real estate transaction you are involved in (e.g., buying a home, selling a home, refinancing a mortgage).

- What are your fees? Be sure to ask about the attorney's hourly rate and how they bill for their services. You should also ask about any hidden fees or costs.
- What is your approach to representing clients? Ask the attorney about their communication style and how they keep clients informed of the progress of their case. You should also ask about their willingness to negotiate on your behalf.
- What are your availability and response time? Find out when the attorney is available to meet with you and how quickly they respond to phone calls and emails.
- Can you provide references? Ask the attorney for references from previous clients. This can give you a good idea of the attorney's reputation and the quality of their work.

In addition to asking these questions, it is also important to pay attention to your gut feeling during the interview. Do you feel comfortable with the attorney? Do you trust them to represent your interests? If the answer to either of these questions is no, it is best to move on to another interview.

Here are some additional tips for interviewing potential real estate attorneys:

- Be prepared. Before your interview, take some time to gather your thoughts and write down a list of questions you want to ask. This will help you to stay focused during the interview and ensure that you get all of the information you need.
- Be honest and upfront. Be honest with the attorney about your needs and goals. This will help the attorney to better serve you.

- Don't be afraid to ask questions. No question is too small or too silly. If you don't understand something, be sure to ask the attorney to explain it to you in plain English.
- Don't feel pressured to hire the first attorney you interview. Take your time and interview several attorneys before making a decision.

3. Choose an attorney you feel comfortable with: Choosing an attorney you feel comfortable with is one of the most important steps in finding and working with a real estate attorney. You will be working closely with this attorney throughout your real estate transaction, which can be a complex and stressful process. It is important to choose someone you trust and feel at ease with.

Here are some tips for choosing a real estate attorney you feel comfortable with:

- Interview potential attorneys. When you are interviewing potential attorneys, be sure to ask questions about their experience, qualifications, and fees. You should also ask about their approach to client communication and their style of practicing law.
- Pay attention to your gut instinct. When you are meeting with potential attorneys, pay attention to your gut instinct. Do you feel comfortable with them? Do you trust them? Do you feel like they understand your needs and goals?
- Choose an attorney who is a good fit for your personality and communication style. Some attorneys are more formal and reserved, while others are more informal and approachable. Choose an attorney whom

you feel comfortable communicating with and who you feel understands you.

- Consider the attorney's fees. Real estate attorneys can vary widely in their fees. Be sure to get a fee agreement in writing before you start working with an attorney. This will help to ensure that you understand the attorney's fees and how they will be billed.

It is also important to choose an attorney who is experienced in the type of real estate transaction you are involved in. For example, if you are buying a home, you should choose an attorney who has experience with residential real estate transactions.

Once you have chosen a real estate attorney, be sure to communicate with them regularly and ask questions if you have any concerns. Your attorney is there to help you and represent your interests in your real estate transaction.

Here are some additional tips for working with a real estate attorney:

- Be honest and transparent with your attorney. Your attorney needs to know all of the facts about your real estate transaction in order to provide you with the best possible legal advice. Be sure to disclose any potential conflicts of interest or any other relevant information to your attorney.
- Be prepared to answer your attorney's questions. Your attorney will likely have a lot of questions for you about your real estate transaction. Be prepared to answer these questions honestly and accurately.
- Respond to your attorney's communications promptly. When your attorney contacts you, be sure to respond

promptly. This will help to keep the process moving forward.

- Keep your attorney updated on the progress of your real estate transaction. This will help your attorney to stay on top of things and to provide you with timely legal advice.

Once you have chosen a real estate attorney, you can start working together to review and understand your real estate contract and to protect your legal interests in the real estate transaction.

10.4. How to find and work with a real estate accountant

To find and work with a real estate accountant, you can follow these steps:

1. Ask for referrals: Asking for referrals is one of the best ways to find a qualified real estate accountant. This is because referrals come from people who have already worked with the accountant and can give you firsthand feedback on their experience.

When asking for referrals, be sure to ask specific questions about the accountant's experience, qualifications, and fees. You should also ask about the accountant's personality and work style. This will help you to find an accountant who is a good fit for your needs.

Here are some specific questions you can ask when asking for referrals for a real estate accountant:

- Do you have any experience working with a real estate accountant?
- If so, who would you recommend?

- What was your experience working with them like?
- Were they knowledgeable and helpful?
- Were they responsive to your questions and needs?
- Did they help you to save money on your taxes?
- Would you recommend them to others?

Once you have a few referrals, be sure to interview each accountant before making a decision. This will help you to get to know the accountant and to determine if they are a good fit for you.

Here are some tips for interviewing potential real estate accountants:

- Be prepared. Before the interview, take some time to think about your needs and expectations. What are your financial goals? What kind of services are you looking for?
- Ask questions. During the interview, be sure to ask the accountant about their experience, qualifications, and fees. You should also ask about their approach to real estate accounting and their philosophy on customer service.
- Be honest. Be honest with the accountant about your financial situation and your investment goals. This will help the accountant to provide you with the best possible advice.
- Trust your gut. After the interview, take some time to think about your feelings about the accountant. Did you feel comfortable with them? Did you feel like they understood your needs? If you have a good feeling about the accountant, then they may be the right fit for you.

2. Interview potential accountants: Interviewing potential accountants is an important step in finding the right one for your real estate business. You want to choose an accountant who is experienced in real estate accounting, has a good reputation, and is a good fit for your personality and business style.

Here are some tips for interviewing potential real estate accountants:

- Ask about their experience. How many years of experience do they have in real estate accounting? What types of real estate businesses have they worked with? What are their specialties?
- Ask about their qualifications. Are they a certified public accountant (CPA)? Do they have any other relevant certifications or training?
- Ask about their fees. How do they charge for their services? What are their typical fees for different types of accounting services?
- Ask about their availability. How often will they be available to answer your questions? How long will it typically take them to complete your tax returns?
- Ask about their communication style. How do they prefer to communicate with their clients? Do they send regular updates? Are they responsive to emails and phone calls?
- Ask for references. Can they provide you with references from other real estate clients?

In addition to these general questions, you may also want to ask more specific questions about your specific business needs. For example, if you are a real estate syndicator, you may want to ask about their experience with real estate syndications. Or, if you own rental properties, you may want to ask about their experience with rental property accounting.

Once you have interviewed a few potential accountants, take some time to compare them and choose the one who is the best fit for your business.

Here are some additional tips for interviewing potential accountants:

- Prepare a list of questions in advance. This will help you to stay focused during the interview and to make sure that you ask all of the important questions.
- Be prepared to answer questions about your business. The accountant will want to learn more about your business in order to assess your needs and to determine if they are a good fit for you.
- Be honest and upfront about your budget. The accountant will need to know how much you are willing to spend on accounting services in order to provide you with an accurate estimate.
- Trust your gut. If you feel comfortable with an accountant and you believe that they are qualified to handle your accounting needs, then go with them.

3. Choose an accountant you feel comfortable with: Choosing a real estate accountant that you feel comfortable with is one of the most important steps in finding and working with a qualified professional. This is because you will be working closely with this accountant throughout the year to manage your real estate finances and to prepare your tax returns. It is important to choose someone you like and respect, and someone that you can trust with your financial information.

Here are some tips for choosing a real estate accountant that you feel comfortable with:

- **Ask for referrals:** Talk to your friends, family, colleagues, and other real estate investors to get referrals for real estate accountants. This is a great way to find accountants who have a good reputation and who are experienced in working with real estate investors.
- **Interview potential accountants:** Once you have a few referrals, interview each accountant to see who is the best fit for you. Be sure to ask about the accountant's experience, qualifications, fees, and communication style. You should also ask about the accountant's personality and whether you feel like you can get along with them.
- **Trust your gut:** Ultimately, the most important thing is to choose a real estate accountant that you trust. If you feel good about the accountant and you feel like they can help you achieve your financial goals, then that is the most important thing.

Here are some questions you can ask yourself to help you choose a real estate accountant that you feel comfortable with:

- Do I feel like I can trust this accountant with my financial information?
- Do I feel like I can get along with this accountant?
- Do I feel like this accountant understands my financial needs and goals?
- Do I feel like this accountant is knowledgeable about real estate accounting?
- Do I feel like this accountant is responsive to my questions and concerns?

If you answered yes to most of these questions, then you have likely found a real estate accountant that you feel comfortable with.

It is also important to note that you do not have to stick with the first accountant you choose. If you are not happy with your accountant, you can always switch to a different one. There are many qualified real estate accountants out there, so you should be able to find one that is a good fit for you.

Once you have chosen a real estate accountant, you can start working together to set up your accounting system, track your income and expenses, and prepare your tax returns.

Here are some tips for working with a real estate accountant:

1. Be organized. Keep good records of all of your real estate income and expenses. This will make it easier for your accountant to prepare your tax returns and provide you with accurate financial information.

2. Communicate regularly. Meet with your accountant regularly to discuss your financial situation and to get advice on how to minimize your taxes. Keep your accountant updated on any changes to your real estate investments or your financial situation.

3. Trust your accountant. You have chosen your real estate accountant because you trust them. Trust them to do their best to represent your interests and to help you achieve your financial goals.

By following these tips, you can build a successful relationship with your real estate accountant and achieve your real estate investment goals.

Here are some additional tips for finding and working with a real estate accountant:

1. Look for an accountant who is certified in public accounting (CPA). This means that the accountant has met certain educational and experience requirements and has passed a rigorous exam.

2. Ask about the accountant's experience with real estate accounting. For example, ask about the accountant's experience with rental properties, fix-and-flip properties, and real estate syndications.

3. Get a fee agreement in writing before you start working with the accountant. This will help to ensure that you understand the accountant's fees and how they will be billed.

4. Ask the accountant about their availability. Make sure that the accountant will be available to answer your questions and prepare your tax returns on time.

By following these tips, you can find and work with a qualified real estate accountant who can help you manage your real estate finances and minimize your taxes.

Chapter 11: Real Estate Investing Success Stories

11.1 Real estate investing success stories from ordinary people

Here are some real estate investing success stories from ordinary people:

Sean Conlon

Sean Conlon was born and raised in a small town in Ireland. He came from a humble background and his family struggled to make ends meet. When he was 18, he moved to the United States to start a new life. He worked hard and eventually saved up enough money to buy his first investment property.

Conlon continued to buy and sell investment properties, and eventually built a multi-million-dollar real estate portfolio. He is now a successful real estate investor, author, and speaker. He has helped thousands of people achieve their real estate investing goals.

Melanie Bajrovic

Melanie Bajrovic was a bartender who was struggling to make ends meet. She dreamed of financial freedom, but she didn't know how to achieve it. One day, she decided to start investing in real estate.

Bajrovic started by buying a small rental property. She worked hard to fix it up and rent it out to tenants. She then used the rental income to buy more investment properties.

Within a few years, Bajrovic had built a multi-million-dollar real estate portfolio. She retired from her bartending job and now lives off of her rental income. She is also a successful real estate investor, author, and speaker.

Elisa Covington

Elisa Covington was a yield manager who was working a regular 9-to-5 job. She was bored and unfulfilled, and she dreamed of a better life. One day, she decided to start investing in real estate.

Covington started by buying a small fixer-upper property. She rented out the second bedroom to help pay for the mortgage. She then used the rental income to buy more investment properties.

Eventually, Covington quit her job and became a full-time real estate investor. She now owns a multi-million-dollar real estate portfolio and generates a significant amount of passive income. She is also a successful real estate investor, author, and speaker.

These are just a few examples of ordinary people who have achieved success through real estate investing. It is possible to achieve your real estate investing goals, regardless of your background or experience. All it takes is hard work, dedication, and a willingness to learn.

Brandon Turner

Brandon Turner was a broke college student when he started investing in real estate. He used his student loans to buy his first investment property, a duplex. He rented out one unit and lived in the other to save money.

After graduating from college, Turner continued to invest in real estate. He bought and sold single-family homes, rental properties, and commercial properties. He also started a successful podcast and blog about real estate investing.

Today, Turner is a multi-millionaire and one of the most respected real estate investors in the world. He is the author of several books on real estate investing and the co-founder of BiggerPockets, a popular online community for real estate investors.

Joe Fairless

Joe Fairless was a high school dropout who was working as a waiter when he started investing in real estate. He used his savings to buy his first investment property, a single-family home. He rented out the property and used the rental income to buy more investment properties.

Within a few years, Fairless had built a multi-million-dollar real estate portfolio. He quit his job as a waiter and became a full-time real estate investor. He now teaches others how to invest in real estate and is the host of the popular podcast "The Best Ever Real Estate Investing Advice."

Grant Cardone

Grant Cardone was a struggling salesman when he started investing in real estate. He used his commission checks to buy his first investment property, a single-family home. He rented out the property and used the rental income to buy more investment properties.

Cardone continued to invest in real estate and eventually built a multi-billion-dollar real estate portfolio. He is now one of the most successful real estate investors in the world. He is also a successful author, speaker, and entrepreneur.

These are just a few examples of ordinary people who have achieved success through real estate investing. It is possible to achieve your real estate investing goals, regardless of your background or experience. All it takes is hard work, dedication, and a willingness to learn.

11.2. What you can learn from these success stories

There are many things we can learn from the success stories of ordinary people who have achieved success through real estate investing. Here are a few of the most important lessons:

1. Real estate investing is possible for everyone. You don't need to be a millionaire or have a special background to get started in real estate investing. Many successful real estate investors started with very little money and experience.

2. Hard work and dedication are essential. Real estate investing is not a get-rich-quick scheme. It takes hard work, dedication, and perseverance to build a successful real estate portfolio.

3. Education is key. Before you start investing in real estate, it is important to educate yourself about the process. There are many books, articles, and online resources available to help you learn about real estate investing.

4. Start small. You don't need to buy a mansion as your first investment property. Start with a smaller, less expensive property. This will help you to reduce your risk and learn the ropes of real estate investing.

5. Be patient. Real estate investing is a long-term investment strategy. It takes time to build a successful real estate portfolio. Don't get discouraged if you don't see results immediately.

Here are some additional lessons we can learn from the success stories of real estate investors:

1. Focus on cash flow. When choosing investment properties, focus on properties that will generate positive cash flow. This is the most important factor in determining the success of your investment.

2. Reinvest your profits. When you start generating profits from your rental properties, reinvest the profits into buying more investment properties. This will help you to grow your portfolio and increase your income exponentially.

3. Build a team. As your real estate portfolio grows, it will be important to build a team of professionals to help you manage your properties. This team may include a real estate agent, a property manager, and an accountant.

4. Don't be afraid to fail. Everyone makes mistakes, especially when they are starting out. The important thing is to learn from your mistakes and move on.

Real estate investing can be a great way to generate wealth and build a secure financial future. By following the lessons learned from the success stories of real estate investors, you can increase your chances of success.

Remember, real estate investing is a long-term game. Don't get discouraged if you don't see results immediately. Just keep working hard, learning, and reinvesting your profits, and you will eventually achieve your goals.

11.3. How to replicate their success in your own real estate investing journey

To replicate the success of real estate investors like Sean Conlon, Melanie Bajrovic, Elisa Covington, Brandon Turner, Joe Fairless, and Grant Cardone, you can follow these steps:

1. Set clear goals. What do you want to achieve with real estate investing? Do you want to generate passive income, build a long-term investment portfolio, or retire early? Once you know your goals, you can develop a plan to achieve them.

2. Educate yourself. There is a lot to learn about real estate investing. Read books, articles, and blog posts. Take courses and attend workshops. Talk to other real estate investors. The more you know, the better prepared you will be to make sound investment decisions.

3. Develop a niche. What type of real estate are you most interested in? Single-family homes? Multifamily properties? Commercial properties? Fix-and-flip properties? Rental properties? Once you have chosen a niche, you can focus your research and investment efforts accordingly.

4. Find a good team. As your real estate portfolio grows, you will need a team of professionals to help you manage your properties. This team may include a real estate agent, a property manager, an accountant, and a lawyer. Choose people who are experienced, knowledgeable, and trustworthy.

5. Be patient and persistent. Real estate investing is a long-term investment strategy. It takes time to build a successful portfolio. Don't get discouraged if you don't see results immediately. Just keep working hard, learning, and reinvesting your profits, and you will eventually achieve your goals.

Here are some additional tips for replicating the success of real estate investors:

1. Focus on cash flow. When choosing investment properties, focus on properties that will generate positive cash flow. This is essential for covering your expenses and building equity in your properties.

2. Invest in yourself. Reinvest your profits into buying more investment properties, educating yourself, or hiring a team of professionals to help you manage your portfolio.

3. Be disciplined. Don't let emotions get in the way of your investment decisions. Make sound financial decisions based on your research and analysis.

4. Be flexible. The real estate market is constantly changing. Be prepared to adapt your strategy as needed.

Real estate investing can be a great way to generate wealth and build a secure financial future. By following the steps and tips above, you can increase your chances of success.

Remember, there is no one-size-fits-all approach to real estate investing. What works for one investor may not work for another. The most important thing is to develop a plan that is right for you and to stick to it.

Chapter 12: The Future of Real Estate Investing

12.1. The trends that are shaping the future of real estate investing

The real estate industry is constantly evolving, and new trends are emerging all the time. Here are some of the key trends that are shaping the future of real estate investing:

1. The rise of smart homes and technology

The rise of smart homes and technology is one of the key trends that is shaping the future of real estate investing. Smart homes are homes that are equipped with devices that can be controlled remotely using the internet or a smartphone app. These devices can include things like thermostats, lights, security systems, and even appliances.

Smart homes offer a number of benefits to both homeowners and renters. For homeowners, smart homes can help to save money on energy bills, improve security, and make life more convenient. For renters, smart homes can make their rental properties more attractive and can help them to charge higher rent.

The rise of smart homes is being driven by a number of factors, including:

- The increasing affordability of smart home devices
- The growing popularity of the internet of things (IoT)
- The increasing demand for convenience and security

The smart home market is expected to grow significantly in the coming years. This growth will be driven by the factors listed above, as well as by the increasing adoption of smart home devices by businesses and governments.

The rise of smart homes is having a major impact on the real estate industry. Investors who are able to identify and capitalize on this trend will be well-positioned to succeed in the years to come.

Here are some of the ways that real estate investors can capitalize on the trend of smart homes:

a. Invest in properties that are compatible with smart home technology. This could include properties that have high-speed internet access, wired or wireless home automation systems, or other features that make it easy to install and use smart home devices.

b. Market properties to buyers who are interested in smart home technology. Many buyers are now looking for homes that have smart home features or that are compatible with smart home technology. Investors can highlight these features in their marketing materials and reach out to potential buyers who are interested in smart homes.

c. Partner with companies that specialize in smart home technology. Investors can partner with these companies to offer their tenants discounts on smart home devices or to provide them with assistance with installing and using smart home technology.

By taking these steps, real estate investors can capitalize on the trend of smart homes and attract more buyers and tenants.

Here are some specific examples of smart home technology that is impacting the real estate industry:

a. Smart thermostats. Smart thermostats can learn your heating and cooling preferences and adjust the temperature accordingly. This can help to save money on energy bills and make your home more comfortable.

b. Smart lights. Smart lights can be controlled remotely and can be programmed to turn on and off at specific times. This can improve security and convenience.

c. Smart security systems. Smart security systems can be monitored remotely and can send alerts to your smartphone if there is a break-in or other security issue. This can give you peace of mind and help to protect your home and belongings.

d. Smart appliances. Smart appliances can be controlled remotely and can be programmed to perform tasks at specific times. This can save you time and energy.

These are just a few examples of the many ways that smart home technology is impacting the real estate industry. As smart home technology continues to develop and become more affordable, it will have an even greater impact on the industry. Real estate investors who are able to identify and capitalize on this trend will be well-positioned to succeed in the years to come.

2. The growing demand for sustainable properties

The growing demand for sustainable properties is one of the key trends that is shaping the future of real estate investing. There are a number of factors that are contributing to this trend, including:

a. Increased awareness of environmental issues: Consumers are becoming increasingly aware of the environmental impact of their choices. This includes the impact of their homes and businesses. As a result, they are looking for sustainable properties that are energy-efficient and environmentally friendly.

b. Government incentives: Governments around the world are offering incentives to promote the development of sustainable properties. These incentives can include tax breaks, grants, and rebates.

c. Lower operating costs: Sustainable properties often have lower operating costs than traditional properties. This is because they use less energy and water. Lower operating costs can lead to higher rental income and resale value for investors.

The growing demand for sustainable properties is creating a number of opportunities for real estate investors. Investors can capitalize on this trend by:

a. Investing in existing sustainable properties: There is a growing inventory of sustainable properties on the market. Investors can purchase these properties and rent them out or sell them for a profit.

b. Converting existing properties into sustainable properties: Many existing properties can be converted into sustainable properties. This can be done by adding features such as solar panels, rainwater harvesting systems, and green roofs. Investors can convert their own properties or they can partner with other investors to convert properties.

c. Developing new sustainable properties: Investors can develop new sustainable properties from the ground up. This can be done by using sustainable building materials and construction methods. Investors can also develop sustainable communities that include amenities such as green spaces and public transportation.

Investing in sustainable properties can be a good way to generate income and capital appreciation. It can also be a way to make a positive impact on the environment.

3. The increasing popularity of co-living and co-working spaces

Co-living spaces are shared living arrangements where residents rent private rooms while sharing common areas such as kitchens, bathrooms, and living spaces. Co-living spaces offer a number of benefits to residents, including:

- Affordability: Co-living spaces are often more affordable than traditional apartments, especially in high-cost areas.
- Community: Co-living spaces provide residents with a built-in community of other professionals and entrepreneurs.
- Convenience: Co-living spaces often offer amenities such as on-site laundry, fitness centers, and co-working spaces.

Co-working spaces are shared workspaces where professionals can rent a desk or office space on a short-term or long-term basis. Co-working spaces offer a number of benefits to professionals, including:

- Flexibility: Co-working spaces offer flexible work arrangements, so professionals can choose to work when and where they want.
- Community: Co-working spaces provide professionals with the opportunity to connect with other professionals in their field.

- Amenities: Co-working spaces often offer amenities such as high-speed internet, printers, and conference rooms.

There are a number of reasons why co-living and co-working spaces are becoming increasingly popular. One reason is the rise of the gig economy and the remote workforce. More and more people are working remotely, and they need affordable and convenient places to work and live.

Another reason for the popularity of co-living and co-working spaces is the changing demographics of the workforce. Millennials and Gen Z are more likely to value experiences over possessions, and they are looking for living and working arrangements that are flexible and affordable.

Real estate investors can capitalize on the trend of co-living and co-working spaces by investing in properties that can be converted into these types of spaces. They can also partner with companies that specialize in managing co-living and co-working spaces.

Here are some specific examples of how real estate investors are capitalizing on the trend of co-living and co-working spaces:

1. Redeveloping old office buildings: Some investors are redeveloping old office buildings into co-working spaces. This is a cost-effective way to create new co-working spaces in prime locations.
2. Converting old hotels into co-living spaces: Other investors are converting old hotels into co-living spaces. This is a way to create new co-living spaces in desirable neighborhoods.

3. Building new co-living and co-working spaces: Some investors are building new co-living and co-working spaces from scratch. This allows them to create spaces that are specifically designed for the needs of their target market.

The trend of co-living and co-working spaces is expected to continue to grow in the coming years. Real estate investors who are able to capitalize on this trend will be well-positioned to succeed in the future.

4. The growth of the metaverse

The metaverse is a virtual world that is still in its early stages of development, but it has the potential to revolutionize the real estate industry. In the metaverse, people will be able to buy, sell, and rent virtual properties. This could open up a whole new market for real estate investors.

There are a number of reasons why the metaverse is expected to have a major impact on real estate investing. First, the metaverse is growing rapidly. In 2022, the global metaverse market was valued at $1139.55 million, and it is projected to reach $15698.24 million by 2030. This rapid growth is being driven by a number of factors, including the increasing popularity of virtual reality (VR) and augmented reality (AR) headsets.

Second, the metaverse is attracting a large and diverse user base. In 2022, there were an estimated 27 million active metaverse users, and this number is expected to grow significantly in the coming years. The metaverse is attracting a wide range of users, including gamers, social media users, and businesses.

Third, the metaverse is becoming increasingly decentralized. This means that there is no single company or entity that controls the metaverse. This decentralization is creating new opportunities for real estate investors. For example, investors can now buy and sell virtual land on decentralized marketplaces such as Decentraland and The Sandbox.

Real estate investors can capitalize on the growth of the metaverse in a number of ways. One way is to invest in virtual land. Virtual land can be used to build a variety of virtual properties, such as homes, businesses, and entertainment venues. Virtual properties can then be rented out to other metaverse users or sold for a profit.

Another way to invest in the metaverse is to invest in companies that are developing metaverse real estate platforms. These companies are building the infrastructure that will support the future metaverse real estate market. Investors who invest in these companies early could stand to make significant profits as the metaverse grows.

Overall, the growth of the metaverse is a key trend that is shaping the future of real estate investing. Real estate investors who are able to identify and capitalize on the opportunities in the metaverse will be well-positioned to succeed in the years to come.

Here are some specific examples of how real estate investors are already capitalizing on the growth of the metaverse:

1. Virtual land development: Some real estate investors are buying and developing virtual land in the metaverse. This land can then be rented out to other metaverse users or sold for a profit.

2. Metaverse real estate investment funds: Some companies are launching metaverse real estate investment funds. These funds allow investors to invest in a portfolio of virtual properties.
3. Metaverse real estate consulting: Some real estate investors are providing consulting services to businesses that are looking to enter the metaverse. These services can include help with acquiring virtual land, developing virtual properties, and marketing virtual properties.

The metaverse is still in its early stages of development, but it has the potential to revolutionize the real estate industry. Real estate investors who are able to identify and capitalize on the opportunities in the metaverse will be well-positioned to succeed in the years to come.

5. The increasing use of blockchain technology

Blockchain technology is one of the most important trends that is shaping the future of real estate investing. Blockchain is a distributed ledger technology that allows for secure, transparent, and tamper-proof transactions. This has the potential to revolutionize the real estate industry in a number of ways.

Here are some of the key benefits of using blockchain technology in real estate investing:

a. Streamlined transactions: Blockchain can be used to streamline the real estate transaction process by automating many of the manual tasks involved, such as title searches, escrow, and closing. This can save time and money for both buyers and sellers.

b. Increased transparency: Blockchain can be used to create more transparent and efficient markets by providing real-time access to data on property ownership, sales history, and other relevant information. This can help to reduce fraud and make it easier for buyers and sellers to find the best deals.

c. Reduced costs: Blockchain can help to reduce the costs associated with real estate transactions by eliminating the need for intermediaries, such as title companies and escrow agents. This can save money for both buyers and sellers.

d. New investment opportunities: Blockchain is also creating new investment opportunities in the real estate industry. For example, investors can now invest in fractional ownership of properties or in real estate-backed tokens. This allows investors to access the real estate market with less money and to diversify their portfolios.

Here are some specific examples of how blockchain technology is being used in real estate investing today:

a. Property tokenization: Property tokenization is the process of converting a physical property into a digital token that can be traded on a blockchain. This allows investors to buy and sell fractional ownership of properties or to invest in real estate-backed tokens.

b. Smart contracts: Smart contracts are self-executing contracts that are stored on a blockchain. They can be used to automate many of the steps involved in a real estate transaction, such as title transfers, payments, and escrow.

c. Decentralized finance (DeFi): DeFi is a new financial system that is built on blockchain technology. DeFi platforms allow users to borrow, lend, and trade assets without the need for intermediaries. This can be used to finance real estate investments or to generate income from real estate assets.

Overall, blockchain technology has the potential to revolutionize the real estate industry by making it more efficient, transparent, and accessible. Investors who are able to identify and capitalize on this trend will be well-positioned to succeed in the years to come.

These are just a few of the key trends that are shaping the future of real estate investing. Investors who are able to identify and capitalize on these trends will be well-positioned to succeed in the years to come.

12.2. How to prepare for the future of real estate investing

To prepare for the future of real estate investing, you should:

1. Educate yourself about the trends that are shaping the industry. This includes the rise of smart homes, the growing demand for sustainable properties, the increasing popularity of co-living and co-working spaces, the growth of the metaverse, and the increasing use of blockchain technology.

2. Invest in properties that are compatible with these trends. For example, if you believe that smart homes are the future, you should invest in properties that are compatible with smart home systems. If you believe that sustainability is important to buyers, you should invest in properties that have sustainable features.

3. Partner with professionals who can help you manage your investments. This includes real estate agents, property managers, and accountants.

4. Be prepared to adapt to change. The real estate industry is constantly evolving, so it is important to be flexible and adaptable.

5. Have a long-term investment horizon. Real estate investing is a long-term game, so don't expect to get rich quickly.

Here are some additional tips for preparing for the future of real estate investing:

1. Focus on cash flow. This is the most important factor in determining the success of your investment. Look for properties that will generate positive cash flow, even after you factor in all of your expenses.

2. Reinvest your profits. When you start generating profits from your investments, reinvest them into buying more properties. This will help you to grow your portfolio and increase your income exponentially.

3. Diversify your portfolio. Don't put all of your eggs in one basket. Invest in a variety of properties in different locations. This will help to reduce your risk.

4. Be patient. Real estate investing is a long-term game. It takes time to build a successful portfolio. Don't get discouraged if you don't see results immediately.

By following these tips, you can prepare for the future of real estate investing and increase your chances of success.

Here are some specific actions you can take to prepare for the future of real estate investing:

1. Start learning about smart home technology and how it can be implemented in real estate. There are many online resources and courses available to help you get started.

2. Research sustainable real estate features and how to make your properties more sustainable. This could include things like solar panels, rainwater harvesting systems, and energy-efficient appliances.

3. Look into investment opportunities in co-living and co-working spaces. These are growing asset classes with a lot of potential.

4. Start learning about the metaverse and how to invest in virtual real estate. This is a new and emerging market, but it has the potential to be very disruptive.

5. Research blockchain technology and how it is being used to develop new real estate platforms. This technology could revolutionize the way real estate transactions are conducted.

By taking these actions, you can position yourself to be successful in the future of real estate investing.

12.3. How to stay ahead of the curve in the real estate investing market

To stay ahead of the curve in the real estate investing market, it is important to be constantly educated and informed about the latest trends and developments. Here are some specific tips:

1. Read industry publications and blogs. There are many great resources available to help you stay up-to-date on the latest news and trends in the real estate industry. Some popular publications and blogs include:

- National Association of Realtors (NAR)

- BiggerPockets
- Inman News
- Real Estate Coach
- The Real Deal

2. Attend industry events. There are many industry events held throughout the year where you can learn from experts and network with other investors. Some popular events include:

- NAR Annual Conference & Expo
- BiggerPockets Real Estate Conference & Expo
- Inman Connect
- Multifamily Executive Conference
- ICSC RECON

3. Network with other investors. One of the best ways to learn about new trends and opportunities is to network with other investors. You can do this by attending industry events, joining online forums, or simply reaching out to people you know who are involved in real estate investing.

4. Use data and analytics. There are many data and analytics tools available that can help you make informed investment decisions. Some popular tools include:

- CoStar
- RealPage
- Zillow
- Trulia
- Redfin

5. Work with experienced professionals. If you are new to real estate investing, it is a good idea to work with experienced professionals, such as a real estate agent, property manager, and accountant. These professionals can help you avoid

common mistakes and make sure that you are making sound investment decisions.

By following these tips, you can stay ahead of the curve in the real estate investing market and increase your chances of success.

Here are some additional tips for staying ahead of the curve in the real estate investing market:

1. Be open to new ideas. Don't be afraid to try new things and invest in new asset classes. As the real estate market evolves, so should your investment strategy.
2. Be flexible and adaptable. The real estate market can be unpredictable, so it is important to be able to adapt your strategy as needed. Be prepared to change your plans if necessary.
3. Be patient. Real estate investing is a long-term game. Don't expect to get rich quickly. Be patient and build your portfolio over time.

By following these tips, you can stay ahead of the curve in the real estate investing market and achieve your investment goals.

Conclusion

Real estate investing can be a great way to generate wealth and build a secure financial future. However, it is important to be educated about the process and to start small. By following the tips and advice in this book, you can increase your chances of success as a real estate investor, even if you are on a budget.

Here are some key takeaways from the book:

1. Real estate investing is possible for everyone. You don't need to be a millionaire or have a special background to get started. Many successful real estate investors started with very little money and experience.

2. Hard work and dedication are essential. Real estate investing is not a get-rich-quick scheme. It takes hard work, dedication, and perseverance to build a successful real estate portfolio.

3. Education is key. Before you start investing in real estate, it is important to educate yourself about the process. There are many books, articles, and online resources available to help you learn about real estate investing.

4. Start small. You don't need to buy a mansion as your first investment property. Start with a smaller, less expensive property. This will help you to reduce your risk and learn the ropes of real estate investing.

5. Be patient. Real estate investing is a long-term investment strategy. It takes time to build a successful real estate portfolio. Don't get discouraged if you don't see results immediately.

If you are serious about becoming a successful real estate investor, I encourage you to take action today. Start by educating yourself about the process and by developing a plan.

Then, take small steps towards your goal of buying your first investment property.

Remember, real estate investing is a journey, not a destination. There will be setbacks along the way, but it is important to keep moving forward. With hard work, dedication, and perseverance, you can achieve your real estate investing goals and build a secure financial future for yourself and your family.

I wish you all the best on your real estate investing journey!